DMITRY RYBOLOVLEV

ARNAUD RAMSAY

DMITRY RYBOLOVLEV
THE MAN BEHIND
MONACO'S
FOOTBALL RENAISSANCE

Biteback Publishing

First published in Great Britain in 2017 by
Biteback Publishing Ltd
Westminster Tower
3 Albert Embankment
London SE1 7SP
Copyright © Arnaud Ramsay 2017

ISBN 978-1-78590-294-9

10 9 8 7 6 5 4 3 2 1

A CIP catalogue record for this book is available from the British Library.

Set in Minion Pro

Printed and bound in Great Britain by
CPI Group (UK) Ltd, Croydon CR0 4YY

MIX
Paper from
responsible sources
FSC® C020471

LIST OF WORKS BY THE SAME AUTHOR

Derrière le sourire, with Antoine Griezmann, Robert Laffont, 2017.

Head High: Confessions of an Enfant Terrible of Rugby, with Mathieu Bastareaud, Robert Laffont, 2015.

Qu'est-ce qui fait courir... Tapie?, drawings by Faro, Jungle!, 2015.

Dans les griffes du Qatar, with Zahir Belounis, Robert Laffont, 2015.

Président Platini, with Antoine Grynbaum, Grasset, 2014.

Champions du monde 98, secrets et pouvoir, with Gilles Verdez, Éditions du Moment, 2014.

Ma mauvaise réputation, with Mourad Boudjellal, La Martinière, 2013, Points, 2015.

Ligue 1, 80 ans de football professionnel, with Paul Dietschy, Solar, 2013.

Paris vaut bien un cheikh, drawings by Philippe Bercovici, 12 Bis Éditions, 2013.

Perles de foot, Fetjaine, 2013.

Laurent Blanc, la face cachée du Président, Fetjaine, 2012.

Ce si gentil David Douillet, Éditions du Moment, 2011.

Anelka par Anelka, Hugo & Cie, 2010.

Jean d'Ormesson ou l'élégance du bonheur, Le Toucan, 2009.

Énergie positive, with Charles Beigbeder, Le Toucan, 2008.

Bixente, with Bixente Lizarazu and Jacques Bungert, Grasset, 2007.

Snake, with Youri Djorkaeff, Grasset, 2006.

Terrain miné: football, la foire aux illusions, with Boris Ngouo, Michel Lafon, 2004.

ARNAUD RAMSAY

English-language edition adapted and updated by Glenn Moore.

To Martin, Amélie and their beloved Papou

CONTENTS

CONTENTS

PREFACE

Imagine a studio of scriptwriters, brought together by a producer keen to develop a feature film. Bottle-fed on the Hollywood approach, they're racking their brains to sketch out an original portrait of the main character and furnish him with flaws. Over the course of some enlightened meetings, the ingredients are intertwined, outlining the meandering path of his unique trajectory, fleshing him out while advancing the plot. At last, after much consideration, his character emerges and the biographical elements are defined in such a way as to better identify with him and follow him on his path.

Anyone reading the resulting synopsis would learn the following: the protagonist is an only child, a boy, born in the mid-1960s at the foot of the Ural Mountains in the USSR, where Leonid Brezhnev has recently become General Secretary of the Central Committee of the Communist Party – a title that has not been used since Stalin. His parents are doctors and 'Mr. X' follows in their footsteps, spending seven years studying cardiology at Perm University, located in his hometown, where his father and mother both teach. While still a student, he marries a classmate and becomes a father at twenty-three. During this period he witnesses the dismantling of his country and the dissolution of the Soviet bloc. Sensing that times are changing, he escapes to Moscow, where he studies economics, before returning home, where he takes advantage of the massive wave of privatisations to create companies and take control of businesses by buying up the vouchers distributed to workers. He purchases one of these companies, which in the space of fifteen years he transforms into a global giant.

It is a success story with its share of disillusionment: eleven months' imprisonment after being accused of arranging the assassination of an associate, as well as the collapse of a mine which swallows up 50 million tonnes of potassium and risks an environmental disaster. While based in Switzerland for his safety, the hero is 'invited' by individuals close to Muscovite power to sell his Uralkali shares, a portion of the capital of which had been listed three years earlier on the London Stock Exchange. At just forty-four years old, he is a billionaire. He travels by private jet, sails his yacht, buys actor Will Smith's villa in Hawaii and the Maison de L'Amitié in Florida from Donald Trump, real estate tycoon and future President of the United States.

In 2011, this man who cultivates discretion and who, officially, claims to speak only Russian is drawn to the glitz and glamour of Monaco and decides to relocate to this captivating place. On Christmas Eve, he suddenly finds himself the chairman of the principality's football club, AS Monaco, which is bottom of Ligue 2. He authorises the spending of millions of euros to strengthen the team and, four-and-a-half years later, wins the Ligue 1 title and reaches the semi-finals of the European Champions League.

Further spicing up this story, which already has a touch of a thriller about it, throw in interminable divorce proceedings and a soon to be ex-wife demanding half of his fortune against a backdrop of trusts in Cyprus and the British Virgin Islands, as well as a legal battle against the world's largest art shipper, from whom he'd bought almost forty paintings for around €2 billion over a ten-year period, and who he now accuses of fraud and money laundering.

So, is it credible or improbable, this fiction apparently concocted by scriptwriters? It's hard to believe, but all of it is absolutely true. Dmitry Rybolovlev – since he is the chairman of AS Monaco in question – exists in flesh and blood. I've even met him.

Without judging Rybolovlev's personality, his fate intrigued me: his mysteries and his secrets, too. Through concentric circles, after long weeks of advance and retreat, I was able to gain access to the man described thus by the Swiss daily newspaper *Le Temps*:

Those who are acquainted with him describe a cold,

changeable creature who is impossible to decipher. Ice man, stone man, snake or even 'endive', the metaphors abound to describe this man of unrivalled intelligence, yet inexpressive, capable of shutting down the slightest hint of emotion on his face. 'He's an infinitely crafty individual, who has admirably manoeuvred in a hostile environment, with great flair for power relations,' explains a person who sat opposite him during his divorce proceedings. 'Behind everything he does, there are ulterior motives.'

The title of the portrait sets the tone: 'The oligarch with a mask of ice.' Or how about the double-page spread in *Libération* in May 2015, which begins as follows: 'Albert II is piqued. The Prince of Monaco has just given an order to the paparazzi: they are banned from photographing him in the company of Dmitry Rybolovlev, the Russian oligarch whose takeover bid on the Rock of Monaco is turning into insider trading.' It matters little that two days before the publication of the article, the billionaire had attended the baptism of Jacques and Gabriella, the five-month-old twins of Albert and Charlène at the Cathédral Notre-Dame-Immaculée in Monaco.

Vanity Fair magazine was in the same camp, dedicating an eleven-page special report to Rybolovlev in its September 2015 issue, 'The Oligarch's Trap', looking back on the conflict that pitted him against art dealer Yves Bouvier. The author states: 'Since his arrival in the principality, four years ago,

Dmitry Rybolovlev has been waiting in vain for the Monegasque passport he requested.'

The image of the big bad Russian was skilfully summarised by journalist Roberto Saviano, author of the bestseller
on the Neapolitan mafia *Gomorrah* – who has since been
living under police protection. In his most recent opus, *Extra
Pure: A Journey into the Economy of Cocaine*, he writes in the
chapter 'The Tsars Conquering the World':

> The Amalfi Coast, Sardinia, Costa del Sol, Tuscany, Malta,
> Ibiza: all of that is Russian!' The person expressing himself
> in these terms knows the difference between the penetrating
> cold of Moscow and the pleasant heat of the Italian coasts
> well. He is a Russian like many others, of the kind who
> invade our country when summer dictates that swimwear
> and sunscreen be worn. They are everywhere and, looking at
> them, we automatically think: Russians, Russian mafia … As
> though all of rich Russia was inevitably criminal.

Dmitry Rybolovlev, while he has retained the soul of his
country in a profound way, does not correspond to the cliché.
His existence makes eyes at the Russian novel instead, the al-
chemy of Russian painting, and the exploration of the depths
of the human soul, showcased by Dostoyevsky, Tolstoy,
Gogol or Bulgakov. If you tell him this, he assents. 'If someone had predicted that I would live such a life, I probably
wouldn't have believed it. Every day, it continues to surprise

me. Yet, sometimes, I ask myself when all of it will calm down a bit.'

This conversation dates from Saturday 16 May 2015, in the lounge of his 1,600m² penthouse on the Avenue d'Ostende, with a view over Port Hercules, the five-star palace L'Hermitage, the casino, and the Prince's palace. A setting procured for €235 million, sold by two British developers, the Candy brothers. Une Belle Époque – the name of the building it is housed within – became infamous when the Lebanese-naturalised Brazilian banker and king of finance Edmond Safra died there after an arson attack in 1999.

Four hours prior to kick-off at Stade Louis II Monaco vs. Metz, on the thirty-seventh match day of Ligue 1, Rybolovlev agreed to meet me at his home. Well, almost his home: the duplex with a circular terrace on the roof, a two-storey library, infinity pool with jacuzzi and spa, games room and movie theatre (which doubles as a 'panic room') has actually been rented for ninety-seven years in the form of a long-term lease. The six-storey building, where HSBC and BNP Paribas each occupy a floor, remains the property of the Monegasque state. Security is discreet but efficient, with bulletproof glass, private elevator, and bodyguards, who escort Rybolovlev to the stadium in a Mercedes van.

Our chat proves to be a litmus test for presenting him with my goal: not a hagiography, not a book of sensational claims, but a scrupulous investigation – already well underway – to establish the story of all of his lives as accurately as possible.

This is a challenge, given how extremely rare his interviews are and the fact that his relationship with the media is almost non-existent. Initially, he forbade himself from becoming a public figure. 'At any rate, I don't consider myself to be one,' he assured me. 'I read the minimum of what might be said about me because it doesn't interest me. Some very tough things are written but I'm used to living with that.'

That is a necessity. Presiding over an historic football club crowned champions of France eight times, or having, according to *Forbes* magazine in 2017, the 190th largest fortune worldwide with $7.4 billion in the bank, inevitably attracts the media spotlight, even if you loathe being caught in its beams.

Between sips of water, calmly seated in his armchair, in dark-coloured casual wear, Rybolovlev listened to me. The translation of our conversation was provided by his faithful lawyer, the Swiss polyglot of Ukrainian origin, Tetiana Bersheda, who also serves on the club's board of directors. Before detailing how I envisioned the book, and telling him I would write it with or without his participation, I briefly outlined my background and explained that I'd ghosted autobiographies for footballers Bixente Lizarazu and Youri Djorkaeff, as well as for Toulon rugby club owner Mourad Boudjellal and its French international Mathieu Bastareaud. I shared my background as a journalist specialising in sport, someone who has covered four World Cups.

Now freelance, my last full-time job had been at *France-Soir*, in 2011. The daily had been taken over two years earlier by billionaire Sergei Pugachev, owner of the delicatessen Hédiard. Nicknamed 'the Kremlin's banker', the former Siberian senator also owned shipyards in Saint Petersburg and liked to frequent Monegasque charity galas; he had set up a chauffeur-driven limousine company in the principality. He gave the newspaper to his 24-year-old son, the French-Russian Alexandre, and established the editorial office at 100 Avenue des Champs-Élysées.

'The best way to lose your money is to buy a club or a newspaper,' I quipped to Rybolovlev, who cracked a smile in spite of himself. At *France-Soir*, I was soon able to catch a glimpse of the owner's cold and direct mentality, of the kind generally attributed to Russians. Handing me a list of staff in the sports department, of which I'd just been named editor-in-chief, he said: 'So, who are we keeping and who are we not keeping?'

Naïve, shy, cynical, and paradoxically likeable, Alexandre Pugachev never went out without his bodyguard. In the end, the failure of *France-Soir* cost the family a lot: a loss of around €80 million and a brand name that disappeared from view after the liquidation of the title and assets sold by the Commercial Court of Paris. In late 2014, Interpol requested the immediate arrest of Sergei Pugachev, in exile in London, and whose foreign holdings had been frozen at the behest of the Russian courts. Moscow claimed $2 billion from him after the bankruptcy of the Mejprombank. Having fallen into disgrace despite having been close to Vladimir Putin, this active member of the Orthodox Church has now taken refuge in Paris.[1]

During a surprising interview in July 2015 with *Le Nouvel Observateur*, Pugachev affirmed having introduced Putin to the daughter of Boris Yeltsin in the late 1990s and even having proposed him as a successor for the top job.

Such are the lives of oligarchs, conveying as many fantasies as they do fears. In any case, Dmitry Rybolovlev does not present himself as an oligarch: he insists he never received any state-owned enterprise and that he only enjoyed the same opportunities as others in the era of privatisations. Over the course of our initial informal meeting, lasting thirty minutes, politics was not mentioned. We talked more about football.

'As a young man in the USSR, ice hockey was the most popular game. I played this sport at school. As for football, I learned to like it,' he confessed.

When Roman Abramovich bought out Chelsea, I went to Stamford Bridge. I wasn't in the presidential grandstand; I wanted to experience the encounter in the midst of the supporters. The emotions I felt that day were very strong. So I understood that one day, I would be the chairman of a football team.

---

1   In September 2015, Pugachev filed international arbitration proceedings in The Hague against the Russian government, claiming $12 billion.

He also evoked his ambitions with AS Monaco, whose slogan under his rule has become 'Like nowhere else', or in the club's shorthand 'Incomparable'.

He said:

> My goal is to be the champions of France once every three or four years – if you never win, ambitious players will no longer sign – and to one day win the Champions League. This season, with the quarter-final against Turin's Juventus, after eliminating Arsenal, showed that we might attain this goal with an intelligent project and a reasonable budget.

'Reasonable' is relative; the budget for 2015–16 was €140 million. Rybolovlev also mentioned his passion for surfing:

> When Uralkali was sold in 2010, I experienced a period where I had a great deal of free time. I tried surfing and I enjoyed it. Nowadays, I don't do it so often but I still enjoy it, all the more since Kelly Slater gave me the board on which he'd become a world champion.

That evening, a week away from the Formula One Grand Prix in the streets of the principality, Monaco won 2–0 against Metz in front of 7,500 spectators, the usual crowd for a venue that can hold 18,500. Not that the empty seats spoil any fun for the man who admits that being alone in a stadium is enough for him, so long as there are emotions to be had.

From his unpretentious box, he watches almost every home match, putting on his glasses, flinching and complaining.

To complete this book, I met with, or questioned, over sixty sources, from Moscow to the principality, via Greece, Switzerland, Perm, Rybolovlev's hometown, and even Berezniki, very near the mines. Given Rybolovlev's reputation, many people refused to answer my questions, while others would only do so anonymously. Let's just say that, between football, Monaco, Russia, and the billionaire circle, Rybolovlev's life verges on the sheer accumulation of secretive milieus!

The modest and discreet Rybolovlev, who turned fifty in late 2016, shut no doors to me and went with the flow, without restricting or encouraging me. This man who loathes interviews also hosted me in the summer of 2015 on his private island of Skorpios, in the Ionian Sea.

My portrait of him does not clear up all the grey areas. But it does shed light on the unusual life of an austere man who nonetheless can still take a joke; a tall man (Rybolovlev stands at 1.85 metres) who, when he gazes at you for the first time, seems to be reading your mind. This strategist, who listens and consults but always has the final say, has no doubt meditated on the maxim, well known in France: 'We only emerge from ambiguity to its detriment.'

CHAPTER 1

PRINCE OF AS MONACO

'**M**onument in danger: buy now.'

If football clubs were advertised for sale in the classified section, like cars are, perhaps this would have been an appropriate headline on an advertisement in the winter of 2011. The text beneath might have read:

> Major football club, currently ranked last in second division, for sale owing to meagre finances, and results in free fall.
>
> The Association Sportive de Monaco Football Club, founded 1 August 1919.
>
> A public limited company affiliated to the French Football Federation under registration no. 91.
>
> Awards: seven-time champions of France (1961, 1963, 1978, 1982, 1988, 1997, 2000), five-time winners of the Coupe de France (1960, 1963, 1980, 1985, 1991), winners of the Coupe de la Ligue (2003). Finalists in the European Champions League (2004) and European Cup Winners' Cup (1992).

Price: €1 (plus debt)

Write to Prince Albert II, c/o Prince's Palace of Monaco.

Obviously, this was not how Dmitry Rybolovlev became owner of AS Monaco on 23 December 2011, in exchange for a symbolic €1, but the description of the club's heritage and crisis is genuine. In its past, Monaco had seen top-flight managers take the helm, including Arsène Wenger, Didier Deschamps, and Claude Puel. It was the club responsible for discovering the phenomenal Thierry Henry, George Weah, and Emmanuel Petit, and its iconic red-and-white shirt had been worn by some of football's biggest stars – Glenn Hoddle, Jurgen Klinsmann, and Youri Djorkaeff. But a decade of decline had brought the club to its knees.

It had always been an isolated club, playing in the French league despite Monaco not being in France itself. The club was predominantly owned by Monegasques through the organisation MSP (Monaco Sport Partenaires). There were only 'locals' involved: 40 per cent for the Société des Bains de Mer, 20 per cent for the Marzocco family, 20 per cent for Patrice Pastor, and 20 per cent for a pool of private shareholders.

However, as football became more expensive, especially in terms of player wages and transfer fees, even the wealthy principality struggled to provide the funds to keep up. With a small population base, many without any natural affinity to the club, AS Monaco attracted meagre crowds. This meant the owners had to make up a shortfall in income. Financial problems led to a forced relegation in 2003 and though that was avoided on appeal, Jean-Louis Campora, who had been president for twenty-eight years, overseeing many triumphs, had to resign.

Improbably, novice manager Deschamps, France's 1998 World Cup-winning captain, steered the club to the Champions League final the following year (losing to José Mourinho's Porto), but that success was illusory. A rapid turnover of chairmen, players and managers contributed to a slide that led to relegation in 2011. When a bad start to Ligue 2 raised the spectre of the club dropping into the regional, part-time ranks, drastic action was required. When you're as glamorous as Monaco, heading for Luçon, Dunkerque, or Les Herbiers in the Vendée (without wishing to insult these locations) lacks spice. Moreover, there was a danger that things get even worse. The spectre of Grenoble loomed. A Ligue 1 club in 2010, a year later Grenoble was put into liquidation and downgraded to CFA 2, the French fifth division.

The club needed a saviour. Fortunately one was at hand, living in Monaco, extraordinarily wealthy, actively interested in owning a football club, and in a position to devote his time and energies to a new challenge. For Dmitry Rybolovlev that project would be reviving *Les Rouges et Blancs*. First, however, he had to persuade the Monegasques, especially the ruler, Prince Albert II, that he was a suitable owner.

Rybolovlev would not be the first Russian owner of a high-profile Western European club. Most notably, Roman Abramovich had bought Chelsea in 2003 and transformed it into a member of the European elite. Chelsea won a series of trophies in England and in 2012 defeated Bayern Munich in the Champions League final.

Abramovich's success was welcome as Monaco had flirted, unsuccessfully, with Russian ownership themselves. For many years, Monaco shirts have borne the name Fedcominvest – a company specialising, coincidentally, in the import and export of the product that made Rybolovlev rich, agricultural fertilisers. In December 2002, Alexei Fedorychev, owner of Fedcominvest, decided he wanted to be more than just the team's sponsor.

A financial backer of AS Monaco (ASM) since 1996, Fedorychev, who also has Hungarian nationality, was living in Monaco in a luxury apartment near the Consulate General of France. Negotiations were proceeding when the principality's then ruler, Prince Rainier, incensed by a revelation in *Le Monde*, abruptly cancelled the takeover bid. The newspaper had published a 1997 memo from the Direction Centrale des Renseignements Généraux (DCRG, French intelligence). Fedcominvest, registered in the tax haven of the Isle of Man, featured in the memo as a 'legal front for organised crime in Western Europe'. The DCRG specified: 'Fedorychev is suspected of being behind an attempt to launder funds originating from weapons and narcotics trafficking organised under the cover of the Monegasque group Galaxy Management, led by mafia boss Leonid Minin,' who was incarcerated in Italy. Just as Campora announced the signing of a memorandum of understanding with Fedcominvest to the players and staff, the Palace intervened to halt the process.

An investigation into Fedcominvest's finances was launched by Monaco's public prosecutor's department, but the probe ended after a year without any action being taken. Fedcominvest continued to sponsor the team. Fedorychev would later become the owner of Dynamo Moscow, which led him to sign a two-year agreement in 2006 with Monaco involving technical exchanges and possible friendlies.

The arrival of Rybolovlev is not comparable with Fedorychev's abortive attempt. 'Rybolovlev went for AS Monaco when the club was no longer attractive. For Russians, Monaco is a prestigious brand, a magical name that sparkles. It is the place to be,' summarises journalist and expert on the country, Pierre Lorrain, whose essay 'L'Ukraine entre deux destins' [The Ukraine: Between Two Fates] was published in 2017. He adds: 'Many wealthy Russians frequent Monaco and the Riviera. It is therefore an ideal calling card in a business context, given that his future was compromised in Russia since he wasn't trusted by the Kremlin.'[2]

According to *Monaco Hebdo*, as of 1 January 2013, 240 Russians over the age of sixteen resided in Monaco, amounting to 0.7 per cent of the total population. Ten years earlier, there had been only thirty-eight. Buying a foreign football club is in vogue among the very rich. Many of England's Premier League clubs

2   Interview with the author.

and second-tier Championship clubs have foreign owners. Apart from Abramovich at Chelsea, the American Glazer family has owned Manchester United since 2005. China's Dr Tony Xia owns Aston Villa, while Singaporean billionaire Peter Lim bought out Valencia in 2014 on the advice of agent Jorge Mendes. Indonesian Erick Thohir, whose fortune was made in publishing and telecommunications, is the major shareholder of Internazionale of Milan, DC.

But being rich does not mean the owners are not also passionate about their clubs, says the expert and consultant in sports economics, Wulfran Devauchelle.

Even if buying a club is a way of penetrating economic or political circles, for Rybolovlev, it is a depreciating investment, particularly due to the barred access for major partners that is unique to Monaco. In France, investing in football is first and foremost a philanthropic act. Gaining profitability or a surplus in value is a challenge. If that was what Rybolovlev was looking for, he would've gone for the English-speaking market. Anyway, the principality didn't have much choice but to sell the club, given its economic situation at the time. It would probably have preferred to sell it to a Monegasque businessman, like Michel Pastor [the real estate mogul and club chairman from June 2004 to April 2008, who died in February 2014, aged seventy], but there were not enough potential buyers back then.[3]

---

3   Interview with the author.

Becoming the chairman of Monaco cemented Rybolovlev's newfound passion for football. Like Abramovich, who was first captivated by Manchester United's 2003 Champions League match with Real Madrid (a 4–3 win for United, but a 6–5 aggregate defeat, in which Brazilian Ronaldo scored a hat-trick and David Beckham netted twice), he fell under its spell at Old Trafford. Rybolovlev says:

> For several months I had a box at Old Trafford. This experience allowed me to gradually improve my understanding of football: the game itself and how things went on behind the scenes. It was hard to travel all the time to follow one team in particular. It was much better to own your own team, and while I was about it, I thought, why not one at home![4]

The star club of Belarus, Dynamo Minsk, was suggested to him, along with its ice hockey section. But when the economic situation of AS Monaco led the Palace to open its capital to new shareholders, Rybolovlev seized the opportunity. It was also a way of signalling that his installation on the Rock would be long term. He claims he had always wanted to live there, given that Switzerland, where he'd been living since 1995, failed to suit him.

'But my wife was against it. When she filed for divorce, I was

---

4   Interview with the author.

finally able to make this dream a reality. The climate, security, sea, quality of life, infrastructure, and the fact that you can get around easily: I love everything about this country,' he affirms.

He had first discovered the principality a few years earlier at the invitation of his friend Vadim Vasilyev, who worked there as a trader during one of his many incarnations (he worked at the Ministry of Foreign Affairs, has been a diplomat at the Iceland Embassy, a sales manager, and owns three restaurants in Moscow). 'I didn't know Monaco and I liked it immediately. I even saw a match at Louis II against Paris Saint-Germain,' recalls the billionaire. And Vasilyev, polyglot and francophone – he used to live in Paris, where his father was a negotiator for the commercial department of the USSR Embassy – is now the vice president and chief executive officer of the club.

Before convincing Prince Albert, Dmitry Rybolovlev had to establish his credentials. Businessman Willy De Bruyn, who has lived in the principality for forty-two years and has received the insignia of Chevalier de Grimaldi,[5] served as a 'Sherpa', a guide in the china shop that is Monaco, where everything is different and more delicate.

The director of the Société des Bains de Mer is a surprising character – De Bruyn is also the honorary consul of Morocco. At seventy-six, the Belgian continues to fly his own twin-engine, medium-haul plane. He travels constantly and knows every inch of Monaco's terrain. Initially introduced through

---

5   Monaco has been governed by the Grimaldi family of Genoese origins since 1297.

Rybolovlev's lawyer Tetiana Bersheda, De Bruyn has advised Rybolovlev since 2010. He serves as a go-between with the Monegasque government and administration.

Their first interaction came as Rybolovlev was on the verge of purchasing the top two floors of the Belle Époque building. 'For this kind of purchase Prince Albert is informed,' notes De Bruyn.

> The government, liaising with France, has the means of investigating the origins of the purchasing funds, which it proceeded to do, if only to verify their legitimacy prior to issuing a long-term visa to a foreign national. Dmitry Rybolovlev jumped through a number of hoops, with nothing abnormal observed at any stage. That didn't surprise me, since he had told me his story and it is an exceptional one. He deserves his success; he is a remarkable manager. And he is much warmer and more relaxed than the iceman image that sometimes comes across. Yes, he likes to laugh, party, and raise a glass. He is very Russian at heart, in the sense that he can have sudden eruptions of joy and friendship.[6]

Although not yet officially his advisor, in the summer of 2011 De Bruyn invited Rybolovlev to the Monaco Yacht Club (YCM), to help him penetrate the mysteries of Monegasque high society. Set up by the Société des Régates, founded in 1953

---

6   Interview with the author.

by Prince Rainier, the YCM is presided over by his son, Prince Albert. A highly select club, the daytime dress code is a navy blue jacket with the pocket adorned with the YCM's coat of arms, a light blue shirt, and a tie featuring YCM motifs.

'We observed the induction of a new member, a ceremony in which Prince Albert presented the certificate,' recalls De Bruyn. 'After the ceremony, I introduced Dmitry to the sovereign, the minister of state,[7] the internal affairs minister, and the president of the Société des Bains de Mer.' The Russian later became a member of the Monaco Yacht Club.

The next step was to approach the football team. 'I had accompanied him to matches in Manchester and I was able to judge how much he loved football,' recalls De Bruyn.

> Giovanni Agnelli, the legendary head of Fiat, and owner of Turin's Juventus, used to say that there are three ways to lose money: with women, the most pleasant way, with gambling, the most exciting, and with a football team, the surest way! But, before taking control of ASM, the process was long and laborious. The Prince hesitated.

This was logical for the man who, in *Nice-Matin* in March 2015, admitted: 'I am first and foremost a supporter before being Prince Albert II. During a match, I'm all worked up. I'm passionate about it.'

---

7   Elected by the Prince, the president of the government council is in charge of the administration of Monaco.

But the club descended into Ligue 2 and since it remained stuck at the bottom of the table, the Palace could only delay the inevitable. Already, in the month of June, after the relegation, Rybolovlev had showed his interest. The principality had turned him down, preferring to keep the team under its own control. But in mid-October, thrashed 4–0 at Guingamp, AS Monaco fell to twentieth place with just one victory in eleven matches. Prince Albert, who watches all home matches, reconsidered his position. A short piece in *L'Équipe* advanced a hypothesis.

'Faced with ASM's drastic descent, the idea of selling the team is back on the cards,' wrote the daily.

All the more so in that the annual €6 million subsidy from the Société des Bains de Mer (SBM), which balances the club's accounts, will end on 31 March 2012 and will not be renewed. Firstly, because, owing to the sluggish economic context, earnings from the SBM's casinos are diminishing. Secondly, because the Monegasque Assembly, which has criticised the management of ASM for several seasons, wants to know how things got so bad for the club.

Potential buyers were hardly tripping over each other. De Bruyn endeavoured to convince Prince Albert that Rybolovlev was the appropriate candidate. Things had to move fast because Monaco would need to recruit during the mid-season transfer window, which was only open in January.

'Once the Prince had agreed, the operation to constitute a group of shareholders and sign with the Monegasque state went very quickly,' De Bruyn remembers. 'It all happened over a weekend.'

It was a weekend in November when De Bruyn finally got the green light. By his side on his mission to influence the sovereign's decision was Jean-Marc Goiran, the founding leader of Jess Group which specialises in the sporting business, particularly the management of players' contracts, and whose premises adjoin Stade Louis II. A close friend of Prince Albert, with whom he watched the 2002 World Cup final in Japan, Goiran is an intermediary with clout in the club, where he moves in the highest circles.

In 2005, I was the assistant manager and then the CEO of Oxford United. Once Prince Rainier died, despite opportunities in the English league, I went home to try to help out ASM. The landscape had changed. That didn't suit the leaders, so I created my organisation, with Fabrice Poullain. Our first major player was Marcelo Gallardo. Leaders came and went and the profits continued to plummet. A messiah was needed to revive the machine because the club was in an unfortunate state. A change of system was required. In May 2011, I met Dmitry Rybolovlev's representatives.[8]

---

8   Interview with author.

Jean-Marc Goiran was invited to dinner at the billionaire's penthouse. He gave Rybolovlev a Monaco shirt which he had been preserving like a relic. The shirt had been worn by Thierry Henry and had previously been in the possession of Louis Allavena, the club's historic storeman.

Goiran stresses:

> I thought it logical to give this gift to the man who was going to restore our hope and pride, at the time our club was close to dropping to the National division and perhaps to extinction … I still don't know if he realises the value of this jersey today for a true ASM supporter.

After the dinner Goiran and Willy De Bruyn, who was also present, worked to alleviate Prince Albert's final doubts. Goiran recalls:

> With Willy, we formed a small lobbying party to try to have our voice heard at the highest level, because many were still thinking that the club should remain Monegasque. Those people were denying the reality of the situation. We worked on that angle, I did my presentation and the idea started to take hold. I didn't have the slightest doubt that Rybolovlev was a passionate man full of good intentions and with extremely sound leadership skills.

The Prince and other interested parties agreed: Rybolovlev

was accepted. From a legal point of view, Rybolovlev 'only' became the chairman and not the owner: the 66.67 per cent of shares he bought belong to Monaco Sport Invest (MSI), a company affiliated to a trust established in Cyprus and whose beneficiaries are Rybolovlev and his two daughters. The ASM, representing the interests of the principality, retains the remaining 33.33 per cent. The Palace, tired of providing endless funding and suffering losses, thus forms a blocking minority.

As soon as he was named chairman of the board of directors, Rybolovlev announced in a statement that MSI had 'committed to investing at least €100 million over the next four years. This amount constitutes a guaranteed minimum and may be increased as required.' For his part, Prince Albert commented that it was inevitable, given the 'financial demands of modern football', to find 'a select partner for development'. In his eyes, this episode had opened up 'a new chapter in the history of the football team so beloved of the principality, which I hope will progressively recover its stature, which in the past made it one of the jewels in the crown of Monaco's sporting life.'

Rybolovlev took over the leadership from Étienne Franzi, head of the CMB, the Compagnie Monégasque de Banque. Among the nine members of the new board, five others besides Rybolovlev were part of MSI: his daughter Ekaterina, his lawyer Bersheda, the ex-manager of Spartak Moscow Evgeny Smolentsev, his close confidant and proxy holder Mikhail Sazonov, and De Bruyn, one of the administrators of the Société des Bains de Mer. It was the first time that the Monegasque government – the principality is a constitutional monarchy with a head of government and head of state – had consented to give investors so much leeway.

Goiran felt it necessary to inject Monegasque blood into the future management team and offered the role of sports director to Youri Djorkaeff. The 1998 World Cup winner, then living in New York, played five seasons for Monaco, winning the Coupe de France in 1991. Goiran imagined his friend Djorkaeff, who had kept a house very near the Rock, in the same role as the Brazilian Leonardo at Paris Saint-Germain: a chic ambassador and networker. Djourkaeff had played in Italy (Internazionale), Germany (Kaiserslautern), England (Bolton Wanderers and Blackburn Rovers) and the US (New York Red Bulls), so he was well connected.

'Youri was up for it. He had the ideal profile: a renowned player, serious connections, bilingual, and highly intelligent. This was the kind of challenge he enjoys,' Goiran affirms. 'He met with the Prince because we had been asked to prepare an organisation chart. My role? I could easily see myself as the go-between for the new leadership and the Monegasques, as a kind of assistant vice president.'

Djorkaeff met Rybolovlev twice for informal discussions, one taking place by chance at Bagatelle in New York where the Russian was celebrating his birthday. Goiran had in mind for head of administration the former goalkeeper, David Ducci, who later became CEO of Amiens and part of the backroom staff when Ivory Coast won the Africa Cup of Nations in 2015. As coach Goiran envisaged Argentinian Marcelo Gallardo, who spent four seasons in Monaco winning the title in 2000. El Muñeco, 'the Doll', was at that time coach of Nacional Montevideo, taking them to the title in Uruguay. Goiran scheduled a telephone appointment with the Prince, who insisted on thanking him: 'HSH is very keen to maintain his good relationships with former players and made this known to the new owner,' said Goiran.

Despite this encouragement, once elected chairman Rybolovlev thought differently. In January 2012, he selected a close confidant, Smolentsev, to be executive director. The latter handled the recruitment during the transfer window, but his stay, best remembered for his authoritarianism, was brief and he left as early as March.

A year later another Russian was made executive director: Konstantin Zyryanov, who came from the business world. In charge of setting up the commercial organisation, he only lasted seven months. The first sports director also had a short-lived tenure. This was Tor-Kristian Karlsen, a Norwegian who came via various European clubs such as Watford, Bayer Leverkusen and Zenit Saint Petersburg (where Smolentsev, then manager of Spartak Moscow, had spotted him). Arriving in March 2012, Karlsen was in charge of recruitment of the professional team, and of the training centre. Six months on he found himself elected executive director, but in February 2013 he quit for 'personal reasons'.

At that time, circumstances and events in my life meant that I couldn't sacrifice myself exclusively to my work. I regret it, but life is unpredictable,' says Karlsen.

I liked working with Dmitry Rybolovlev. He's a strategic, approachable, intelligent, reasonable, and fair-minded leader, gifted with a highly tuned analytical mind. We had a direct relationship that meant that decisions were made quickly. Today, he bases the growth of the club on the talents of the training centre and on recruiting young foreign players with strong potential, the most logical and effective way to lead a team.[9]

The Norwegian, now a consultant, remembers Rybolovlev's support,

including when I made mistakes, which is the sign of strong and modern management. We didn't always agree but he was the boss and he legitimately had the last word. Football is an environment in perpetual motion where you're constantly having to make decisions. In 2012, the club reorganised itself in a frenetic manner, for the leadership roles as well as on the field. That sometimes led to errors. In these cases, rather than criticising me, Rybolovlev supported me, pointing out that this experience would be useful. People often have false ideas

9   Interview with the author.

about Russians, who are perceived as pitiless and authoritarian creatures.

Another Russian also assumed a key role on the managerial team. Olga Dementyeva has been the administrative director since June 2012. Discreet and efficient, speaking both French and English, she spent four years at Uralkali before becoming responsible for hospitality and protocol at the club.

It is unsurprising that Rybolovlev often chose to employ people he trusted and whom he had worked with before. But this waltz of leaders with a strong Russian component dismayed Jean-Marc Goiran. 'I was obviously disappointed because I had enthusiasm for my favourite club and wanted the best for it,' he said.

> I had suggested that they incorporate locals, from the very particular Monegasque microcosm. What makes a club prestigious is its history. And who makes that history, if not the players? They chose a different option, but I understand that Rybolovlev wanted to run the club himself. He needed a period of adaptation.

Another Russian joined the dance. Dmitry Chechkin had worked with Rybolovlev for seven years at Uralkali, the potash company where Rybolovlev made his fortune. Hired as vice president of ASM in March 2012, Chechkin quit the following September. He now lives in Portugal with his family and has not forgotten the state in which the club found itself.

'It's simple: the situation was catastrophic on a financial level and in terms of organisation. The management was not very well handled. Dmitry Rybolovlev took a risk becoming the chairman of Monaco. In the beginning, around him, no one knew about or really understood football,' insists Chechkin, who includes himself among that bunch.

> The chairman was attentive to the slightest detail, pouring over every dimension, from the turf to the players' housing, and discussions with the coach. He asked a lot of questions and didn't stop doing so until he'd understood. Knowing that he was rich, many agents abused this and raised the stakes. At first he suffered, then he adapted. He also devoured books in Russian on the history of football and biographies on players. As soon as he took over the club, he watched all the matches and devoted all his time to it.[10]

Among those Rybolovlev went to for advice on players and directors was Konstantin Sarsania. The coach of Lithuanian club Atlantas Klaipeda since 2013, Sarsania had enjoyed a moderate playing career that began with Dynamo Moscow and ended at Dunkerque. He had then been an agent and sports director at Zenit Saint Petersburg. 'I sometimes

---

10   Interview with the author.

crossed paths with him in Moscow through friends we have in common,' says Sarsania of Rybolovlev.[11]

> As he didn't know much about football prior to Monaco he asked me quite a few questions. He was curious, interested, and absorbed all sorts of information, before digesting it and forming his own opinion. He likes to know everything about a case before deciding. He exudes intelligence and soon filled in the gaps in his knowledge. He knows how to listen and be patient, while others, on the grounds that they're rich, are persuaded that they already know everything.[11]

When Chechkin left Monaco the club recruited its technical director from Italy. Riccardo Pecini, director of the AC Milan training centre, had previously been a scout for Fiorentina and Tottenham. His role was to coordinate and supervise the team, the training centre, recruitment, and the medical unit.

Not all of the leaders quit. Belgian Filips Dhondt increasingly became part of the master plan. Before moving to the principality, Dhondt had roamed about the football world; his first experience had been as general manager of Cercle Bruges KSV. He had been a coordinator of Euro 2000, jointly staged by Belgium and the Netherlands and won by France, and had then spent nine years at FC Bruges, the city's star club. Elected the executive director of Zulte Waregem, which

---

11   Interview with the author.

he reorganised, he then dashed off to Hungary to occupy the same position at Újpest Dózsa in Budapest.

On 26 December 2011, three days before Dmitry Rybolovlev bought Monaco, Dhondt received a call from a mutual Russian contact. The next day, Dhondt met Rybolovlev in the Swiss ski resort of Courchevel.

'We talked for an hour and a half; I explained my background, he revealed his ambitions with ASM to me. "I want to win the Champions League," he assured me. I looked at him with wide eyes because Monaco was at the bottom of the Ligue 2 table,' relates the Belgian. 'Then he added: "I know that this will take time but, one day, I want to win that competition." We talked about the project and strategy. He asked me to start at the principality from the first of January.'[12]

Dhondt was not able to start that quickly, but secured his release from Újpest Dózsa and began his new adventure on 13 January. He became managing director, in charge of administrative, commercial, and organisational matters, the commercialisation of Stade Louis II and relations with the French footballing authorities.

The Belgian was one of the first French-speakers among the leadership. He found it amusing that, for a while, sixteen different nationalities occupied the offices: Monegasque, French, Italian, Russian, Belgian, Portuguese, Finnish, English, Dutch, Norwegian, Serb, American, etc. English was the functional

---

12   Interview with the author.

language. These days, although the club remains international, not to mention its players, everyone (or almost everyone) can get by in French. In addition, since the summer of 2014, the deputy director general has been Nicolas Holveck, recruited from AS Nancy-Lorraine, where he was vice president. Vasilyev, No. 2 at ASM, speaks perfect French, as does his advisor, as that has been Dhondt's position since September 2014.

The latter expressed his desire to take some time out, as his family were still in Belgium. But he hasn't forgotten his first steps on the Rock. 'I started on Friday with a meeting with the chairman at his home, to discuss the transfer window, which would be over at the end of the month. At 11 a.m., he invited me to participate in another meeting,' Dhondt recalls.

> I didn't know where we were going. It transpired that we were going to the Palace to have a chat with Prince Albert. That lasted nearly two hours, and I was impressed by the Prince's football knowledge. As for Rybolovlev, I soon noticed that, in meetings, he always asks the right question and gets straight to the point. This is then transformed into a fast decision-making circuit.

Dhondt appreciates 'complicated challenges' and he got his fair share. 'At first, the commercial and communication departments didn't exist. There was no team management either. The infrastructure needed to be rebuilt and improved.' Dhondt doesn't say it, but it's clear that a casual, village-like atmosphere had previously been the norm. However, things were destined to change. An indication of the new professionalism was that wearing an ASM suit would become compulsory at evening matches.

But football is not only determined in offices. On the field, after the dismissal of Laurent Banide in September 2011, the team was coached by one of the club's former strikers. Not Gallardo, despite Goiran's hopes, but the Italian Marco Simone, who was trained by AC Milan and also spent time at Paris Saint-Germain. It was an odd choice as Simone had even less experience than Gallardo of whom Goiran still says: 'I think and hope that one day Marcelo, a highly gifted player, will become the coach of ASM.'[13]

Since retiring as a player Simone had been a director at Legano, an agent, and a marketing consultant for Monaco. At the Prince's request he accepted the challenge of becoming coach. He was thus coach when the first transfer window of the Rybolovlev era opened. It was a vitally important window for the club and ten players were signed between 1–31 January 2012.

This window is never an easy time to sign players. Most are under contract and clubs do not want to let their good players go. Monaco ended up signing a multi-national collection, mostly of relative unknowns such as German

---

13   Coach of River Plate since 2014 Gallardo led the Argentinian club to win the two most prestigious competitions in South America, the Copa Sudamericana, and the Copa Libertadores.

Andreas Wolf, Greek Georgios Tzavellas, Uruguayan Gary Kagelmacher, Dutch player Nacer Barazite, and Hungarian Vladimir Koman. Two players who signed were still under contract: the surefooted international goalkeeper, Croatian Danijel Subašic, and the Belgian-Moroccan attacking mid-fielder Nabil Dirar, bought for €7.5 million from FC Bruges.

But while there was chaos behind the scenes and a welter of introductions required at the training ground, a change often has the effect of shaking a club out of its torpor. ASM had not won any of their last ten matches, but the inaugural game of the Rybolovlev era ended with a victory in Istres, on 14 January 2012, thanks to a goal from emblematic captain Ludovic Giuly. That Saturday evening among the 3,484 spectators in the Parsemain stadium (not even a quarter-full) was Dmitry Rybolovlev.

'Before the match, I'd joined him in his box, which was probably about four to five square metres,' recalls Dhondt.

It was freezing. We were in the midst of a discussion when he suggested: 'Filips, let's have a shot of vodka.' I replied: 'I'd love to Chairman, but I've never drunk vodka.' He handed me a shot saying 'nasdrovia', meaning 'cheers'. I answered in English that it was good. And he replied: 'Not good, it is the best.' That was the real Rybolovlev: comfortable and smiling.

That first win provided confidence and momentum. ASM now played ten matches in a row without defeat, including

five consecutive victories, and discovered a wonderful striker in Senegal's Ibrahima Touré, the scorer of eight goals in
twelve games. Touré had been spotted in the United Arab
Emirates by Jean-Luc Buisine, a former defender who had
built up a great reputation as the head of the recruitment
unit in Lille. Arriving on the Rock in July 2011, Buisine sur-
vived until 2013 when he moved to Rennes. He confided to
L'Équipe that when Rybolovlev and his management group
arrived 'we felt that, for them, all the incumbents were bad.
We were all brushed aside.' Buisine, however, was able to pull
one rabbit from the hat with Touré.

'The new leaders had to "produce" a striker and had been
unable to,' Buisine recalled.

> Simone, a great guy who I had told to believe in this player,
> had talked about Touré to Evgeny Smolentsev, the then exec-
> utive director, who authorised me to recruit Touré. For the
> first two matches, Touré played two fifteen-minute spells and
> at that stage, it all came down on me like a ton of bricks:
> 'That player's useless, a disaster.' After that, something clicked
> and he scored goal after goal. During my second season,
> the chairman asked me to go give my advice about Barce-
> lona–Milan, Brazil–Russia, and in London, etc. I've always
> been impressed with Rybolovlev. I felt that he was heavily
> involved. He was always asking pertinent questions.

Monaco raised their game and ended the season eighth,

after having believed for a crazy moment that they might even return to the elite of Ligue 1, so good had their form been. Despite difficult circumstances, Simone had done well. But Rybolovlev felt that winning promotion to the top flight would require a more experienced coach. This was to be a man who had suffered one his biggest coaching disappointments at the hands of Monaco.

Claudio Ranieri knew all about Russian owners. He had been manager of Chelsea for three years, gradually overhauling the team, developing defender John Terry and signing midfielder Frank Lampard. After Roman Abramovich bought the club in 2003, Ranieri spent £120 million that summer, bringing in players such as Claude Makelele, Joe Cole, Damien Duff, and, less successfully, Juan Sebastian Veron and Hernan Crespo. That season Chelsea finished runners-up, their best league finish for forty-nine years, and progressed further than ever before in the Champions League. However, all season Ranieri had been dogged by well-sourced rumours that his job was under threat. So much so that, despite knocking London rivals Arsenal out of the Champions League, by the time the semi-finals came along he was widely regarded as a 'dead man walking'.

The semi-final was against Monaco, coached by former Chelsea player Didier Deschamps and, unbeknown to most people, a club in as much financial trouble as Chelsea had been prior to Abramovich's takeover. Chelsea were doing fine in the principality as the closing stages approached, drawing

1–1 with Monaco down to ten men. But Ranieri gambled on winning the tie, substituting a striker for a defender, and Monaco took advantage to win 3–1. A 2–2 draw in the second leg of the tie at Stamford Bridge, with Spain's Fernando Morientes inspiring a Monaco comeback from 2–0 down, sealed Ranieri's fate.

Since then the Italian had managed Valencia, Parma, Juventus, Roma and Internazionale, with success at times but no major trophies. He was now sixty, a coach for twenty-six years, though not previously in France. While he had never won a major league title (and would not do so before leading Leicester City to their famous Premier League success of 2015–16), he had been promoted three times as a player and three times as a manager. Promotion was Monaco's goal. Tor-Kristian Karlsen recalls:

> We needed a charismatic, experienced man capable of providing a solid defensive line, of implanting a victors' mentality in a short space of time, while training a group of newcomers (given how fast the turnover had been) comprising around twenty nationalities. Added to this was the fact that the team's physical condition was mediocre. For all of these reasons, Ranieri fitted the bill perfectly.

All the same, his compatriot Roberto Mancini, who had not yet extended his contract at Manchester City after winning the Premier League, was approached first. Mancini decided to stay at City (who would sack him at the end of the season after losing the FA Cup final to relegated Wigan Athletic).

During his first press conference, Ranieri, ever-charming, got the audience on side. When a journalist asked him if he could get by in French, Ranieri answered: 'Hello, I'm Catherine Deneuve.' Unsurprisingly, his audience burst out laughing. He went on to explain that he had just seen an advertisement for a car in Italy in which the actress said this in French.

Joking aside, Ranieri would have no excuses for not regaining Ligue 1 status. Monaco provided him with the means, recruiting Argentinian Lucas Ocampos for €11 million, the most expensive second division transfer. With Valère Germain, Yannick Ferreira Carrasco, Touré, Mounir Obbadi, Andrea Raggi, Dirar, and Kagelmacher also proving influential, Monaco led Ligue 2 from start to finish.

Promotion was secured two matches from the end, after a victory during added time, in Nimes, on 11 May 2013. Present at the Costières Stadium, Rybolovlev, usually undemonstrative, could not contain his delight. He went to congratulate the players in the changing room before taking off in his private plane. Now he could move to the next level. Names such as Cristiano Ronaldo, David Beckham, and Radamel Falcao were in the Russian's mind.

But, behind the scenes, ASM's troubles were not over. Two months earlier, the French League's board of directors had decreed that all professional teams must domicile their head office in France as of 1 June 2014 or face exclusion. It was a clear message directed at Monaco. The advantages conferred on the club by Monaco's generous income tax rates (zero for foreign players, very low for French ones) had long been an issue with some rivals. Bringing matters to a head was the pledge by new French President Francois Hollande to introduce a 75 per cent tax rate on earnings above €1 million.[14] This would clearly have a damaging impact on the competitiveness of French clubs compared to elsewhere in Europe; indeed, the clubs briefly threatened to strike. It would also further expand the taxation gap between Monaco and the rest.

In his message of congratulation, Frédéric Thiriez, president of the *Ligue de Football Professionnel* (LFP), commented on its website: 'The return of ASM among the elite, with a powerful and solid shareholder, is good news for L1. Monaco is in its rightful place within the French football league. It is therefore all the more vital that ASM conform to French regulations at the fiscal level, so that equality across the championship is preserved.'

This was the same Thiriez who, although trophies for the champions of Ligue 1 and Ligue 2 are traditionally presented at the clubs' home stadiums in front of the fans, waited until 13 June, well after the end of the season, to award Rybolovlev his trophy. The event took place almost on the quiet, at the

---

14   The supertax rate was reduced to 50 per cent in December 2012 after a court ruling was dropped in December 2014.

Hôtel de Paris, on the Rock, in the presence of the minister of state of the principality, the secretary of state, and the state councillor. Well-versed in delivering speeches, the LFP president[15] trotted out a tribute to the team, 'which only lost once during the second half of the season: practically invincible'. By way of conclusion, Thiriez issued a message: 'While there is much talk about the special situation of Monaco at present, I am certain that a solution can be found. I am confident in the wisdom of men.'

---

15   On 15 April 2016, Frédéric Thiriez announced his immediate resignation, one
      month after announcing that he would not be seeking a second mandate.

CHAPTER 2

SECRET OPERATION: A TIGER ON THE ROCK OF MONACO

Promotion secured, the next target was a signing to show Europe that Dmitri Rybolovlev, and Monaco, meant business. Rybolovlev aims high and he set his sights on the most recognisable footballer of the century's first decade, and on a world footballer of the year. When neither of those two transfers happened – and a newly promoted Ligue 1 club with an average crowd of less than 10,000 is not the most attractive proposition – Rybolovlev went for one of Europe's deadliest goal scorers. This was Radamel Falcao, and Monaco saw off stiff opposition to sign him.

But first, the two who got away. David Beckham was nearing the end of an illustrious career which had seen him win 115 England caps as well as league titles and cups in England with Manchester United, in Spain with Real Madrid, and in the US with Los Angeles Galaxy. There had also been two spells at AC Milan. Rybolovlev hoped the 37-year-old would be tempted by one last challenge in another new country, with the additional bait of a location possessing all the necessary attractions to lure his wife, Victoria, the former Spice Girls singer turned fashion designer.

Contact was made in November 2012, with Monaco already looking bound for a top-flight return. Beckham still had a handful of weeks left in the US which is where CEO Tor-Kristian Karlsen discreetly met him. ASM offered Beckham a six-month contract to lead their young team, plus a one-year option, in the event of the anticipated rise to Ligue 1. Talks with the Englishman's entourage lasted a month, during which Galaxy won a second MLS Cup, the main American title.

Finally, on 26 December, Monaco abandoned the chase. When Karlsen resigned the following month (for unconnected personal reasons) he admitted his 'surprise' that the Beckham discussions had mainly revolved around the financial aspects instead of, as he'd hoped, 'around the project, play or tactics'. That, he said, 'was why it never resulted in anything concrete'.

TKK, aged forty, a former recruiter for Swiss (Grasshopper Club Zurich), English (Watford), German (Bayer Leverkusen and Hannover 96), Russian (Zenit Saint Petersburg), and Norwegian (Fredrikstad FK) clubs, is now a consultant for various teams in North America, England, and the Arabian Gulf, while also working with *The Guardian*, ESPN, and Norwegian television. He recalled his talks with the Beckham clan.

I spoke with his advisors in Los Angeles as the player was concentrating on the final phase of the MLS, which kicked off the next day, and he intended to focus on the match. Beckham is a wonderful professional and would've been a first-class ambassador for ASM. However, I imagine he'd already been contacted by Paris Saint-Germain. We would've needed a totally incredible offer to convince him to come into Ligue 2.[16]

Beckham had turned down PSG a year earlier for 'family reasons'. This time he signed for the Parisian club on 31 January 2013, the last day of the winter transfer window. He spent five months in the capital, playing fourteen matches in total, enough time to collect another championship medal in another country.

Ronaldo had taken Beckham's place at Manchester United, and then followed the same path to Real Madrid, eclipsing his predecessor at both. By 2012 he was as recognisable as Beckham, and was regarded, along with Lionel Messi, as one of the world's two best players. The pair have been contesting the status of world's best player for most of the second decade of the twenty-first century and although Argentina's Messi has won more Ballon d'Or awards, Rybolovlev regards Ronaldo more highly.

'They are both extraterrestrials but I consider Ronaldo the

---

16   Interview with the author.

better of the two,' he says. 'If you put Messi anywhere other than Barcelona, the result is not guaranteed. Ronaldo doesn't need other people.'[17] Rybolovlev is laudatory about the slick athlete who claims to do 3,000 abdominal exercises per day. The two men have already met. CR7 – Ronaldo's nickname, formed by his initials and shirt number, a trademark that is also the identity of a galaxy, the brightest in the universe, discovered by Portuguese astrophysicists – gave the Russian a replica of his first Ballon d'Or. It is not insignificant either that, in his office, Vadim Vasilyev, vice president and executive officer of AS Monaco, displays a photo of his boss and himself in Ronaldo's company along with a framed shirt signed by the attacking midfielder.

The possibility of luring Ronaldo was rendered credible by the cordial relations struck up between Jorge Mendes and Dmitry Rybolovlev. At the latter's request, Tor-Kristian Karlsen travelled to Madrid in the autumn of 2012 to meet the most powerful football agent in the world. Mendes is close to Ronaldo, very close, being agent, best friend and a godfather to his son all rolled into one.

Ronaldo's apparent dissatisfaction at Santiago Bernabéu, where coach José Mourinho was seemingly at war with not just Barcelona's players and the Spanish media, but also his own Real Madrid players and club management, further encouraged Monaco. With Ronaldo refusing to sign a new

17   Interview with the author.

contract at Madrid, hope lived in Monaco and enough contact was made for rumours to start. In June 2013, with Mourinho on his way out of Madrid but a new deal still to be agreed by Ronaldo, *The Independent* exclusively announced that ASM was going to make a €100 million offer, which would have been the highest fee paid since Ronaldo had left Manchester United for Real Madrid in 2009 for €93.3 million. The English daily also stated the, by then, newly promoted Monegasque club would pay a record salary of €20 million per year, a figure boosted by the knowledge that thanks to the club's special status, non-French players on the team would be exempt from income tax.

On 4 July 2013, at a sponsor's event at the Hôtel de Paris in Monaco, Ronaldo was questioned by *Nice-Matin* about the possibility of moving to the principality permanently. He replied: 'It's a good club with a fantastic owner. I wouldn't say that I would never go to this club, but today, I'm happy at Real Madrid. I just want to go to Monaco on holiday.' Two months later Ronaldo finally signed a new contract at Madrid. The salary did not match that proposed by Monaco, but was nevertheless a substantial increase, and, importantly, higher than Messi's at Barcelona.

While Monaco failed to land Ronaldo the good relations fostered with Jorge Mendes paid dividends. Underlining his status as the sport's prime agent Mendes brokered the arrivals of Radamel Falcao, João Moutinho, James Rodríguez, Ricardo Carvalho, and Fabinho, for a total of €130 million.

The big deal was Falcao, procured from Atletico Madrid for €60 million, the most expensive transfer in the history of Ligue 1.[18] It seems strange to relate that fact to English readers, given Falcao's subsequent struggles at Manchester United and Chelsea, but the South American was once the most highly prized striker in the world. Indeed, he had already scored a treble at Stade Louis II on 31 August 2012, and during the UEFA Super Cup, he scored three times against Champions League winners Chelsea.

That Falcao signed with a promoted team, foregoing the Champions League and conscious that he would be playing in a stadium that is rarely full, came as a complete surprise. Summing up many people's views was the comment Bernard Caïazzo, the head of Saint-Étienne, made at an awards dinner on 19 May 2013. Seeing the vice president of ASM weaving his way through the crowd in front of him, Caïazzo jested to a journalist from *L'Équipe*: 'If Falcao signs with Monaco, I'll buy the Eiffel Tower!' Vasilyev chose to ignore the remark.

Twelve days later Falcao signed for ASM. Caïazzo is yet to submit a bid for the most famous and symbolic monument of Paris. 'It's true, I didn't imagine for a single second that Falcao might come to play in front of 7,000 people,' admits the man who has directed Les Verts since 2004.

---

18   Since then, Falcao's deal has been exceeded by two acquisitions by Paris Saint-Germain: the Uruguayan Edinson Cavani, transferred to Naples for €64 million, and the Argentinian Ángel Di Maria, acquired by Manchester United for €63 million.

At the time, it reminded me of the famous phrase of Mark Twain, the author of *The Adventures of Tom Sawyer*: 'They did not know it was impossible, so they did it.' In any case, well played, Monaco! Thanks to the stir this transfer created, it has contributed to putting the club back on the map.[19]

Caïazzo could be forgiven his error as negotiations were conducted in utmost secrecy. So that Falcao, nicknamed El Tigre since childhood – 'One of my friends compared me to a tiger because my movements on the field were very "hungry". It stuck and I like it' – could become the Monegasque club's poster boy, nothing could be leaked, especially not to the Spanish press. Within ASM itself, the staff were not informed. Rybolovlev and Vasilyev ran the operation in conjunction with Mendes.

Though Atletico needed to cut their budget, Falcao, warned the agent, would be expensive, very expensive. 'We did not expect to invest so much so soon, but the chairman didn't want to miss the unique possibility of recruiting Falcao,' explains Vasilyev. 'Together, we went to his place in Madrid. We obtained the consent of Miguel Ángel Gil Marín, the owner of the team. He specified to Falcao that our project was ambitious and top level.'[20]

The 27-year-old Colombian was interested, but he asked for guarantees. Not financial ones – they would come much

---

19 Interview with the author.
20 Interview with the author.

later – but he aspired to play in a competitive team and to be challenged and supported by excellent players. Rybolovlev asked him who he wanted to have around him. Falcao put forward two names: his Colombian compatriot James Rodríguez and the Portuguese player João Moutinho. Two dribblers with flawless technique who were playing for Porto, one of his former clubs, and for whom Jorge Mendes, as luck would have it, was also the agent.

In March 2013, Rybolovlev and Vasilyev undertook a series of quick trips to Porto. The talks were held in the calm of a trendy inner-city hotel. Mendes, once again, was not far away. Everything was conditional on Monaco's return to Ligue 1. An agreement was struck to acquire James Rodríguez and João Moutinho. Yet still Falcao needed convincing. He requested an appointment with Prince Albert, as a way of reassuring himself and hearing about the viability of the Monegasque appetite from the sovereign's lips. The meeting took place at the Palais de Monaco, overlooking the Mediterranean Sea. Falcao was accompanied by his wife, the Argentinian singer Lorelei Taron, whom he'd met while playing for River Plate, of Buenos Aires. Prince Albert's words placated the striker, who Chelsea and Real Madrid were also courting. Still Falcao needed to be sure. To convince himself that his future lay on the Rock of Monaco, he spent the weekend there with his wife.

'They did a tour of the principality and loved the city. They could also see that we meant business. From then on, with his agent, we really started talking figures about his move,' Vasilyev says. 'And if Falcao's photo was occasionally taken, word didn't spread. In Monaco, it is possible to stay discreet. Besides, the residents are used to seeing stars out and about.'

Monaco agreed the €60 million fee with Atletico (meeting the release clause) and an agreement with Falcao for his salary (€14 million net per season for five seasons). A confidential photo session took place with the Colombian, his compatriot James Rodríguez, and João Moutinho, each with the ASM jersey on their shoulders. The shoot took place in La Turbie, the training centre. The photo would later serve for the season ticket campaign.

The time to reveal Falcao's signing was imminent. It was to be made public at the party celebrating the crowning of the Ligue 2 champions. In front of 2,500 supporters, among the petit fours, aerial acrobatics, autograph and photo sessions, and a concert by American rapper Akon, Claudio Ranieri and his players were warmly applauded. Prince Albert, after thanking him, presented a square ball to Dmitry Rybolovlev, while Konstantin Zyryanov, the chief executive officer,[21] revealed the club's new logo. The Monaco brand name was restored to centre field, with ASM becoming AS Monaco.

But top of the bill was the announcement concerning Falcao. In suit and tie, Dmitry Rybolovlev uncharacteristically took the microphone to say a few words in French read

---

21   Zyryanov left the club in October 2013 just seven months after his arrival.

off a sheet of paper, addressed 'to our dear fans'. He left it to his lawyer, Tetiana Bersheda, in a red dress by his side on the stage, to reveal the rest.

'I had a lot of interesting business projects,' said Rybolovlev.

But now, I have an amazing feeling. That's the passion of football. And this is just the beginning. We must all continue to work a lot harder for the club, continue to grow, win trophies, and contribute to the development of French football. My most fervent wish is to allow our fans to be proud of our club and to bring joy to all football fans, all over the world.

He concluded: 'On this day, I would like to officially announce that Radamel Falcao has signed the agreement with our club.' Thunderous applause ensued, and a video message from El Tigre, proclaiming in Spanish his pride at wearing the red-and-white strip, was played.

As intended, the recruitment of such a star lent the Monegasque project credibility and acted like a detonator, shifting the club into a whole new world. Monaco were back on the sporting map, and not just in Colombia, where interest was so great that the club's Facebook page clocked 125,000 fans.

Falcao, a powerful all-round striker, the scorer of sixteen goals in forty-three appearances for Colombia, had just scored twenty-eight goals in thirty-four matches in La Liga. Previously he had won the Portuguese title with Porto and, almost single-handedly, the Europa League, the latter feat one that he repeated with Atletico. His reputation was to ease the recruitment of other talents, such as two former French internationals also playing in Spain: Éric Abidal and Jérémy Toulalan.

In early July 2013, sporting a stunning salmon suit with a pastel blue shirt, Falcao was presented to the media. The venue had not been chosen lightly: the Belle Époque room of the Hôtel Hermitage, a five-star hotel with a sea view. The club produced the international broadcast signal and offered it free of charge to television channels, so as to better harness the media impact. Rodríguez and Moutinho were introduced first. Then, speaking into a forest of microphones, Falcao was word perfect:

> Knowing that you're going to play a fundamental role in a project gives a player confidence and peace of mind. The conviction of the leaders was also important. The support of the principality, the very firm conviction of the people at the club were decisive factors. The club aims high and I'm central to the project. Many think that it'll be a failure; they might be right, but it's up to me to prove them wrong.

As for the lower attendances at Stade Louis II, in contrast to the fiery fervour of Atletico Madrid's Vicente Calderón and its 55,000 spectators, he insisted he was fine with that. 'A player's motivation has nothing to do with whether the stadium is full or not. With or without an audience, a victory is worth three points. That's a player's primary motivation. It's up to us to motivate people to come.'

A recruit who knew all about Monaco's small gates was Abidal. Finalist in the 2006 World Cup, triple champion of France with Lyon, and winner of a string of titles with Barcelona, Abidal's glittering career had begun on the Rock. He made his Ligue 1 debut with Monaco at nineteen years of age. Now he had returned, eleven years after leaving. He saw it as an opportunity to come full circle (though he would actually finish his career with a brief sojourn at Olympiakós in Greece), and, he said, 'as a way of thanking the club for enabling me to be a professional footballer.'

Abidal added: 'The project was attractive as the objective was to play in the Champions League the following year. The club did everything it could to achieve its goal, especially through recruitment. It was vitally important to make its way up the ranks.'[22] Of Rybolovlev he said:

He is discreet, but does a great deal of work in the shadows. Our first meeting took place at a lunch at his home, along with Vadim Vasilyev. That was where I discovered his charisma and imposing presence. I was very surprised by his humility. The gamble has already paid off. Just look at how the team has progressed.

---

22   Interview with the author.

Abidal joined another experienced signing to the Monegasque defence: the Portuguese player Ricardo Carvalho. He arrived from Real Madrid after impressing Vasilyev with his 'reliable, professional and ambitious personality' during a clandestine meeting in the player's Jeep. This elegant player was thirty-five and had suffered from injury problems, but he had a champion's pedigree, having won many medals with Porto and Chelsea under José Mourinho, and then collected more silverware in Spain.

Carvalho was also from Jorge Mendes's stable. Vasilyev acknowledged this apparent dependence had raised eyebrows, but stressed Monaco were benefiting.

> Mendes is an excellent professional. Agents serve their own interests, that's only natural, but he has a human side to him and builds relationships of trust. He was always fair to us. Nobody believed we'd get Ricardo Carvalho. He persuaded me that the opposite was true. It's true we picked five players from Mendes in the first year because there was also twenty-year-old Fabinho, who was on loan to us and not expensive. I was able to take a risk because no one knew him. But it paid off and now he's playing for the Brazilian team. Mendes is a man of his word.

On loan for two years to the Portuguese team Rio Ave, right-back Fabinho is now under contract with Monaco until 2019. On 2 July 2015, 37-year-old Ricardo Carvalho extended his contract for another season with Monaco. In later years there would be others bearing the Mendes seal of approval, such as the loan for 2015–16 of Fábio Coentrão, the vastly experienced left-back from Real Madrid. His arrival compensated for the departure of 22-year-old international Layvin Kurzawa, trained in Monaco and sold for €24 million to Paris Saint-Germain, whose overwhelming financial muscle – and desire to flex it – had by then come to dominate the French transfer market.

While Falcao changed everything about the perception people may have had about the principality's club, his impact on the pitch was dogged by bad luck. He began well, scoring on the opening day of the championship in Bordeaux. He also scored a point-saving equaliser at the Parc des Princes against Paris Saint-Germain, which kept Monaco top of Ligue 1. After nineteen league and cup matches, Falcao had scored eleven goals. He was also showing good form for Colombia, scoring nine times in qualifying to propel them to the 2014 World Cup finals.

But, on 22 January 2014, in a Lyon suburb, Falcao's season came to a shattering end.

The Coupe de France is the only domestic cup competition in the world to challenge the FA Cup for drama, history, and romance. While not as old, having begun in 1917, it is open to many more teams than the FA Cup – itself fabled for including teams of butchers and bakers along with elite professionals. While entry to the FA Cup usually numbers around 750 clubs, the Coupe de France features more than 8,000. Like the FA Cup there are giant-killing feats and in recent years part-timers have even reached the final.

However, such romance can have a dark side. Amateur players tend to be more rustic in their tackling; their pitches can be rutted and medical facilities limited. Nevertheless Monaco, then second in the league behind PSG, went to Monts d'Or Azergues, from Chasselay, a village in the Rhône department with a population of 2,700, in confident mood. All seemed to be going to plan when Falcao scored. But five minutes before half-time, as he surged into the penalty area seeking a second goal, he was clumsily fouled by opposition centre-half Soner Ertek, a teacher by profession. Falcao's left leg took the weight of the tackle and his knee buckled. No penalty was given, which was surprising given that Ertek made no contact with the ball.

Falcao tried to play on but fell to the ground and, after treatment, was carried off on a stretcher. As the player departed, Ranieri harangued the referee, screaming: 'I told you before.' Afterwards the coach said:

I'm not happy with the referee. It's normal that the Chasselay players were tough, and that something could happen to someone. But there were no cards given. Several times before the injury to Radamel, I spoke to the fourth official that the match was starting to get very physical and that it was getting dangerous for the players. Nobody listened and, not for the first time, we paid the consequences. It's a real shame for French football; the players that play attractive, attacking football don't get enough protection from the referees.

Ranieri added: 'I hope that it's nothing serious for Falcao. If Falcao has a serious injury, it's the referee's fault. It's not possible to let things go like that. When there are fouls, you have to whistle.'

After he arrived that night at Nice airport, while waiting in a transit zone before leaving on a private plane to receive treatment in Porto, the striker received a phone call. 'Thank you, Dmitry,' he said as he hung up. Rybolovlev, speaking in English, had called Falcao to express his support and that of the club.

These words of comfort were consoling, but the verdict was unforgiving. Ranieri and Falcao's worst fears were realised. Scans revealed Falcao had damaged the anterior cruciate ligament in his left knee. He was out, not just for the rest of the season, but would also miss the World Cup in Brazil. Ertek received death threats from Colombia, where Falcao is considered a national treasure.

In Falcao's absence it was Monaco's other Colombian, James Rodríguez, who shone in Brazil. The midfielder dazzled the crowd, making the World Cup quarter-finals and scoring six goals, the best total in the competition. His sequence of chesting the ball down with a pivoting volley to score against Uruguay, in the quarter-finals, was named FIFA's goal of the year.

A few weeks later, Rodriguez was transferred to Real Madrid for €80 million, the fifth most expensive transfer in history. Falcao's ego took a hit, but more problematic was the effect his knee injury appeared to have on his game. Initially he seemed fit, returning late in the 2014–15 season to score twice in three matches. That was enough to persuade his admirers he was back to his best and with Rybolovlev adopting a different strategy, of developing young talent into stars rather than buying ready-made ones, suitors were encouraged.

Manchester United won the chase, securing Falcao on loan for €10 million with a €55 million buyout option. But amid the frenetic pace of the Premier League, Falcao looked a spent force. He scored just four goals and at the season's end United demurred on their option.

Monaco now had a problem: Falcao's contract still had three years to run, his salary was huge, but he did not fit into their new strategy. Falcao was not keen on returning either. The solution, unexpectedly, was to remain in England, with Falcao joining Chelsea. This seemed a surprise, until the dots were joined. Chelsea were managed by José Mourinho, a client, like Falcao, of Jorge Mendes. Part of the deal involved Mario Pašalic, a twenty-year-old Croatian international, being loaned by Chelsea to Monaco.

Again there was a buyout option, this time with a €50 million fee, but again the option was not exercised because, again, Falcao failed. He scored early in the season, in August, but never again as he became an even more peripheral figure at Stamford Bridge than he had been at Old Trafford, a by-stander as Mourinho's season went into meltdown. Injuries were an issue, but the English view was that at thirty, Falcao was, sadly, finished at the top level. This time there were to be no other takers. When Falcao returned to Monaco it seemed it was simply because neither he nor the club had any alternatives.

CHAPTER 3

ORIGINS IN PERM

To Europeans the Ural Mountains have long presented a barrier, a virtual geographical border between two continents, symbolised or even represented by the grandiloquent calls of General de Gaulle in the midst of the Cold War, urging the constitution of a 'Europe from the Atlantic to the Ural'[23] so as to better establish the limits of the old continent. The mountains are not high: the highest peak, Mount Narodnaya, is a mere 1,895 metres (6,217 feet). But this unofficial line of demarcation is long, spanning nearly 2,500 km and dividing Russia from the Arctic Ocean to modern-day Kazakhstan. From the other side, to the east of the Ural Mountains, the huge expanse of Siberia becomes part of Asia.

Perm, however, looks west, initially to Moscow, 1,500 km and a two-hour flight away. Located at the foot of the mountains, Perm has a population of around 1 million and is

---

23 In November 1959 in Strasbourg, General de Gaulle announced to the gallery: 'Yes, it is Europe. From the Atlantic to the Ural, it is Europe. It is Europe, all of Europe, which will decide the fate of the world!'

traversed by the long Kama River, which runs into the Volga and then the Caspian Sea.

Perm was founded in 1723 by Tsar Peter the Great in his quest to develop the Ural region, though the city was briefly renamed Molotov between 1940 and 1957 in a compulsory tribute to the then powerful foreign minister and one of Stalin's most loyal lieutenants: Vyacheslav Molotov. Now Molotov is better known as the man who – through irony as much as mockery – had his name appended to the petrol or alcohol bomb-in-a-bottle used by Finnish soldiers against the invading Soviets in 1939: the Molotov cocktail.

An important industrial and mineral production centre, Perm has a few other historical footnotes. Tsar Nicholas II's younger brother, Grand Duke Michael Alexandrovich of Russia, was assassinated in Perm in 1918 and Boris Pasternak wrote part of *Doctor Zhivago* there.

It was in Perm, on 22 November 1966, that Dmitry Yevgenyevich Rybolovlev was born, the only son of Eugene and Zinaida. His cosy childhood den was an apartment in a working-class neighbourhood. He grew up on the fifth floor of the nine contained in a drab, grey building (in Russia there is no ground floor), five minutes from the city centre. Until recently, the apartment was still owned by Rybolovlev's parents. They had moved to Monaco after retiring, but were letting the flat.

Dmitry's youth, although a lonely time in his life, was also a pampered one. There was not even the slightest problem with his education until he reached the first year of second-ary school. When winter came, a serious case of tonsillitis eventually revealed underlying heart problems. Myocarditis, a form of heart failure of unknown origins, resulted in him being packed off to a sanatorium – to a location in the great outdoors, in a remote village an hour's drive away. Here he received treatment and continued his studies at a less hectic pace.

'The lessons were adapted, lasting, for example, thirty minutes instead of forty-five. During this episode, I could do anything I liked except play sport,' he recalls.

> I did however practise judo for two years, including when I had a sore throat, which may have provoked these heart problems. Before and after the sanatorium, I also played a lot of ice hockey at school. A medical test a few years later showed that I had no after-effects and could play whatever sport I liked. On the other hand, I never played football.[24]

This is not so surprising. Though FC Amkar Perm, a pro-fessional club since 1995, now plays in Russia's top flight and had a brief foray in Europe – losing to Fulham in the Europa League play-off match in 2009 – soccer has never been the focus of sporting life in Perm. In Rybolovlev's youth there was Zvezda Perm, who periodically played in the second tier

---

24   Interview with the author.

of the Soviet League, and the more junior Neftyanik Perm. But both have since folded. The ice hockey club Molot-Prikamye Perm played in the USSR championship's top division for most of Rybolovlev's childhood, though without ever challenging the dominance of the Moscow clubs.

The city was proudest of the feats of the PBC Ural Great Perm basketball team, Russian champions in 2001 and the first non-Muscovite club to win national titles since the dissolution of the former USSR. They went on to win the Russian Cup and the FIBA EuroCup Challenge. However, the club fell victim to financial woes and was shut down in 2009.

The son of doctors, Dmitry Rybolovlev's path seemed laid out for him. 'In my family, all of our conversations revolved around this theme,' he confirms. 'At the time, it was a matter of making the best possible career choice.' It was therefore logical that, after secondary school, he decided to enrol at the Medical Academy of the state of Perm. While the city had an opera school and a ballet school of international standing, it was also highly regarded for the rich diversity of its scientific research institutes, including its Academy of Medicine, founded in 1916.

Rybolovlev was to remain for six years at the academy where his parents, in addition to being consultants at hospitals and clinics, were both teachers. His father, a cardiologist, taught radiology, but Rybolovlev had a somewhat atavistic tendency towards the former. 'I'd always wanted to choose a speciality field related to the heart. It isn't linked to the illness

I'd had aged eleven, but as it turns out, I did develop an interest in this organ very early on,' he says. 'Rather than surgery, which was a possibility, I opted to be an A&E cardiologist. From the second year of classes, I was working nights, as a nurse's assistant. I spent a lot of time reading medical books. I liked studying. I enjoyed that life.' In 1990, he obtained his red diploma, reserved for the most deserving students in each year group.

Since 2005, the rector of the Medical Academy of the State of Perm has been Doctor of Medical Sciences Irina Petrovna Koryukina. This strong, well-groomed woman is particularly proud of her faculty, which now welcomes 3,440 students a year, including eighty foreigners, and has 180 professors. She remembers the long six-year period Rybolovlev spent at the school, and the seventh year that he spent at a partner institution.

'He was a student with a very high level [of ability], formidable intelligence, organised, and methodical. Calm but sociable, he made friends easily. He was 100 per cent involved, as [he is] in everything he does. He was also curious about other subjects, always ready to try new experiences,' she affirms.

Cardiology and reanimation feature among the most complex areas of expertise, but he always did well at those; every year he ranked among the best. He didn't make a big deal about it because he is modest and not the type to blow his own trumpet.

I'm convinced that he would've succeeded in any field. And, to his great credit, he did so quietly ... He soon went into business, but I can guarantee you that he was a good doctor.[25]

She adds: 'I am delighted that one of our former students is so famous. He is no doubt the only person with medical training to have become a billionaire in Russia.'

She believes the medical faculty taught him a few precepts that could also apply to business.

'The level is high and competition intense,' she says.

Being a student here obliges you to be focused, rigorous, responsible, visionary and well organised. It is a school of life. Our academy has produced 50,000 doctors since its creation, but we find some of our former students in all trades, given how unusual the years when Dmitry was studying [the late 1980s] were for Russia.

Although he has long left medicine behind Rybolovlev has remained connected to the university, not least as his parents taught there. He has funded the acquisition of many medical books that take pride of place in the huge library, as well as, through donations, the renovation of an amphitheatre and other rooms (though he refused to allow any of them to bear his name).

---

25   Interview with the author.

In 2010, he returned to Perm to participate in the twentieth anniversary celebrations of his class's graduation. 'Thank God: he has never forgotten us,' the rector chimes. 'He often comes back to see us, and he is informed of everything, particularly via his parents, two highly respected figures. They taught here all their lives. When you know them, having a bad son would quite simply have been impossible.'

Koryukina enjoys giving visitors a tour of her university. Silence reigns, the atmosphere is studious. The maze of corridors and stairwells stretches on and on, until the professors' wall appears, a kind of 'Hall of Fame' for all those who have left their mark at the academy over the last 100 years. Among those whose photographs are displayed there is Eugene Rybolovlev, Dmitry's father, who transmitted his intellectual curiosity to his son and who Dmitry greatly resembles, with his reflective side and silences followed by decisive interventions. From his mother, who is more whimsical and exuberant, it is more her strength of character that Rybolovlev has inherited.

He is very much a combination of the two: as reserved and analytical as his father and as extrovert as his mother, but only in the presence of his close circle.

Irina Petrovna Koryukina confirms and refines this portrait, as she has remained close to his parents. 'His father is very academic. He is a typical Russian professor, with his beard and glasses. He is like a character from Anton Chekhov,' she explains.

He is calm in all circumstances, never raising his voice even if he doesn't agree. He is determined, intelligent and pedagogical, speaking at length with his patients, chatting with them, discussing rather than imposing a point of view. Incidentally, Eugene keeps in touch with them. He is never caught off guard because, in his line of work, he is prepared to react to any situation. He keeps abreast of medical news by reading lots of journals, because he is still passionate about it. Armed with a scientific background, he has a paternalistic side that reassures the students, who still do not hesitate to consult him and ask for his advice. He is retired but is still capable of making diagnoses and continues to work on some research.

This overwhelming enthusiasm, which would be suspect if it did not appear so sincere, the rector also applies to Dmitry's mother, Zinaida.

Now there's a special case! It is rare to meet such a woman. She's a motor that never stops running. She is beautiful, full of energy, always up for having a good time. She is positive, highly organised, buzzing with ideas, didactic like her husband, ready when necessary to lend a hand for her colleagues. She is at the heart of the family: she is its regent, the one who animates its social life. They really are an ideal couple. Everyone loves them.

The Medical Academy of the State of Perm is also where

Rybolovlev met his future wife, Elena Rybolovleva, who was then called Elena Chuprakova. A pretty and brilliant student, with blonde hair and blue eyes, Elena was immediately noticed by Dmitry. 'The first time I saw her she was in the waiting line for enrolment,' he recalls. 'She was just in front of me. We were in the same group for the entrance exam, then again in the same cardiology group. Our six years of studies were spent together.' Just fifteen days separates them: he was born on 22 November 1966, she on 7 December.

Also an only child, Elena's mother was an engineer. It was thanks to her mother's job that, in a period when travelling long distances was uncommon in Russia, Elena travelled around the USSR and neighbouring countries. She first studied mathematics before joining the medical academy, where her and Rybolovlev's love at first sight blossomed into marriage. In their third year at the academy, both aged twenty-one, they exchanged their vows without signing a contract – such a thing did not exist at the time.

'In Perm, each week, we admired ballets at the Opera, visited museums, and went to the theatre. We had a very beautiful love story. An inseparable relationship worthy of the finest Russian novels,' Elena commented in January 2014 to the Swiss economics magazine *Bilan*, in one of her rare confidences.

Two years after exchanging their vows, the couple's eldest daughter, Ekaterina, was born. The two young doctors lived a modest lifestyle in Perm. Factory and manual workers were better paid and respected at the time. To help make ends meet Rybolovlev joined his father in a company specialising in magnetic therapy, a method of treatment, popular in Russia, using magnetic waves. This experience was enough, during the death throes of the Soviet Union, to persuade him that private business, rather than medicine, was his future.

CHAPTER 4

THE TSAR OF POTASH

Despite appearances, Dmitry Rybolovlev laughs loudly and often. He likes to use subtle humour and jokes that catch you out. While you're trying to find out to what extent his teenage reading of the novel *The Financier,* by Theodore Dreiser, may have influenced him, as he has suggested in his sparse interviews, Rybolovlev comes out with:

> I was twelve or thirteen and I was staying with friends of the family. I stumbled on this book, which presented the notions of speculation, the penal code, and the world of business and finance all at once. It was one of the only books available that talked about the mechanisms of the market economy because, during the Soviet era, we hardly knew anything at all about business and its modus operandi. I was inflamed and impressed by it. Two things in the book particularly pleased me: what was said about women and

money. Well, as far as women go, I'm not sure I've completely understood![26]

He then dissolves into a fit of laughter.

Dreiser was born in Indiana in 1871, the son of a German immigrant father and Mennonite mother. His first works, dealing with social inequalities – a sensitive subject in his view – were published to general indifference. *An American Tragedy*, however, struck a chord being adapted for the stage and, twice, for the screen with the 1951 version, starring Montgomery Clift, Elizabeth Taylor and Shelley Winters, winning six Academy Awards. For author Norman Mailer, Dreiser 'came closer to understanding the social machine than any other American writer who ever lived'.[27]

It was in 1912 that Dreiser published the book that shook up Rybolovlev's certainties. *The Financier* was the first volume of what Dreiser called the *Trilogy of Desire*, to which he added *The Titan*, published two years later, and *The Stoic*, published in 1947, two years after his death. The trilogy tells the story of American Frank Algernon Cowperwood and was inspired by the life of transport magnate Charles Tyson Yerkes, who died in 1905. A key figure in the development of the transport systems of Chicago and London, Yerkes

---

26   Interview with the author.
27   Mailer, Norman. Cited in Lingeman, Richard 'The Titan', *American Heritage*, 1993. http://www.americanheritage.com/content/titan (Accessed October 29, 2016).

was no stranger to dubious business methods and neither is Cowperwood.

Dreiser's book is set in Philadelphia, Pennsylvania (also the birthplace of Yerkes). Cowperwood is (like Yerkes) imprisoned for corruption after the Great Chicago Fire of October 1871 exposes his embezzlement of public money. The rest of the story involves prison, the Republican Party, divorce, and then a comeback when Cowperwood again becomes a millionaire thanks to his investments in the global crash of 1873. He then decides to leave Philadelphia and start a new life in the West.

In 1990, after leaving Perm's medical academy, and while still a hospital intern, Dmitry Rybolovlev created his first company, Magnetics. Founded with his father, the company specialised in the therapeutic use of magnets, whose electromagnetic fields were intended to help heal fractures and wounds, reduce pain and combat stress and chronic diseases. Such forms of unconventional medical treatment have existed since ancient times when people believed in the healing powers of naturally magnetic stones. Is it just the placebo effect? It is hard to be categorical; some scientists have voiced doubts. But the Cartesian view is not one that is widely shared in a country where Rasputin, fabled healer of the Russian Imperial family, continues to fascinate long after his savage murder in 1916.

'In the Soviet period, all retail activity was prohibited and considered illegal. By associating himself with his father,

Rybolovlev's sincere aim was to treat people rather than wanting to make money,' says journalist and writer Pierre Lorrain, an expert on Russia.

> Was it quackery to exploit people's credulity? At any rate, the population were very fond of these kinds of things and of unexplained phenomena. At the time, the members of the Politburo did not hesitate to resort to magnetism or use electronic systems. Some of them, to get well, even swallowed special electronic pills, subsequently expulsed in the natural manner. They believed in this very strongly. As for magnetic therapy, I do not know if that has therapeutic virtues. But with this small business, Rybolovlev was able to start to accumulate regular financial income.[28]

Married and now a father, Rybolovlev enjoyed working with his own father, Eugene, who perfected this method of treatment, popular in Russia at the time. Zinaida, Rybolovlev's mother, was never far away.

> As soon as his studies had ended, Dmitry Rybolovlev organised his private company based on medical principles that already existed in Perm. He had learned these at university, given the fact that magnetic therapy techniques are appreciated in Russia, where they continue to exist in certain

---

28   Interview with the author.

hospitals. His father had read and studied a lot on the subject. His mother worked with them,

confirms Irina Petrovna Koryukina, the rector of Perm's medical academy.

With Magnetics, Rybolovlev learned how to do business, getting ahead of the game in a country whose economic revolution was in full swing. The inherent restrictions of the Soviet system were unravelling. Privatisation of the country was underway and there would not be room for everyone. The idea of the greater good no longer existed. Anarchy seemed a heartbeat away.

'The country was undergoing a major shift. Recruitment of employees, renting office space: all of that was new to us,' recalls Rybolovlev. A novice when it came to the market economy, other than what he could glean from *The Financier* which he used as a kind of business manual, he decided to leave for Moscow in 1992 to perfect his knowledge.

In the capital Rybolovlev began an accelerated course in finance. 'I read widely and voraciously. I took classes, notably those on offer at the stock exchange,' he says. Following these sessions, he was awarded a certificate by the Ministry of Finance for securities transactions. More than just a degree, this was an official licence to develop an activity, recognised by the government. He was one of the first to obtain this precious licence.

After returning to Perm, Rybolovlev put Magnetics to one

side and in 1992 opened a brokerage and investment company. At the same time, he launched an auditing company. To protect himself and enable his businesses to continue to grow, he joined forces with a surprising character, twenty years his senior: the former army officer Vladimir Shevtsov who was one of the managers of the property fund for the Perm region, a body managing state-owned assets. This helped Rybolovlev to enter the political field and associate with the big bosses of the region. Together with Shevtsov he created an investment bank.

This period in Russian history was wild and historic. 'We need millions of property owners, not a small group of billionaires,' said Boris Yeltsin when he launched his vast privatisation policies. Yeltsin was the first President of the Federation of Russia, elected on 25 December 1991 by members of parliament following Mikhail Gorbachev's resignation, then elected by universal suffrage the following year. Yeltsin was supported by Anatoly Chubais, a young economist who had become head of the Federal Agency for State Property Management.

Seeking to convert Yeltsin's pledge into reality, the authorities decreed that all citizens could receive a voucher worth 10,000 roubles (around $50) which they could use to buy shares in almost 5,000 businesses that were being privatised. Over 140 million people took advantage of the scheme. Meanwhile the price of staples such as bread was liberalised. Inevitably prices rose exponentially. For the first time, consumers were confronted with the market economy. This reform of ownership, in a country where the government had controlled everything just several months earlier, sent shockwaves through the population: democracy for all in the eyes of some; a massive clearance sale of Soviet industry at bargain prices in the eyes of others.

Dmitry Rybolovlev was interested in the vouchers. Those belonging to workers who could swap shares in exchange for cash, as well as vouchers distributed to the population, who could use them to trade. He and Shevtsov purchased vouchers from workers who wished to sell, and exchanged others for various goods, such as food or cars. This enabled them to get the main businesses in the Perm region to use their bank. 'They then became our customers because, from then on, the central bank authorised the creation of independent banks,' he explains.

This mass privatisation and transition towards a market economy obviously left the way clear for corruption. Companies that had so far belonged to the state were sold for a song and the emerging mafia seized control of them. This crazy period saw the emergence of the infamous oligarchs who saw a unique opportunity to appropriate national wealth, buying the jewels of the country's industry and natural resources, such as oil or gas, at bargain prices then often selling them back in parts and making tremendous profits. The oligarchs were to be the main beneficiaries of 'loans for shares'.

Does Dmitry Rybolovlev fall into this category? He is often

described as an oligarch. He vigorously refutes the term. Questioned by *Paris Match* in November 2013, the billionaire explained: 'I never received a state-owned enterprise. I received from the state the same possibility as all Russians at the time: that of taking shares, at the time of the great wave of privatisations.' Asked what had enabled him to get ahead, he replied: 'Strategic vision. I always try to look further ahead, to make my decisions according to my long-term goals. Then comes tactics and operational management.'

So, is he a real oligarch or isn't he? An informed Russian observer, a member of Russian high society who wishes to remain nameless, is clear: 'Rybolovlev's profile is absolutely no different from others who built their fortunes on the fall of the USSR. If, as criteria for determining who is an oligarch, you refer to the false bankruptcies and other methods of theft for taking control of production capital that the original shareholders divided among themselves, or to government corruption, he is clearly among them.'[29]

However, unlike the more famous oligarchs of the Yeltsin era, such as Mikhail Khodorkovsky, Roman Abramovich, Boris Berezovsky, Vladimir Potanin or Vladimir Gusinsky, Rybolovlev was not simply given the keys to denationalised companies. He was smart, patient, and opportunistic. At a time when it was 'every man for himself', he managed to forge ahead, without the slightest hesitation. He was also

---

29   Interview with the author.

able to get Vladimir Shevtsov on his side to broaden his network.

Russia was forging ahead with all-out privatisation. In the summer of 1994, 15,000 companies were privatised, with the private sector now accounting for over 60 per cent of GDP. The government had naively hoped that people would use their vouchers to build up share portfolios and buy cars to revive the economy. But the voucher scheme proved a disaster. Poorly informed, most Russians who had surfed on the first phase of privatisation did not make any profits. Some lost everything, since many of the new companies were emptied of all their assets. For his part, by buying up as many vouchers as he could get his hands on at very low prices, Rybolovlev became an owner of factories. His investment bank locked into the capital of around twenty companies which transferred their funds to him. These figures grew until he decided to refocus.

From 1994 onwards, he concentrated his efforts on a handful of companies. Among these, one company in particular grabbed his attention: Uralkali, in the mines of the Ural, which produced potassium-based fertilisers, a mineral salt present in many food products and a valuable fertiliser for agricultural use. The company, whose first extraction of potash had begun in 1934, was based 200 km from Perm, in Berezniki, on the banks of the Kama River. Until then, this uninspiring city was most famous for having been the home of Boris Yeltsin for twelve years, after his father, who had just been freed from a labour camp, found work there on a construction site. It was there too that, as a student, Yeltsin lost two fingers on his left hand while trying to defuse a grenade thrown into a church.

The Shevtsov–Rybolovlev duo increasingly invested in Uralkali, which, apart from Berezniki, owned mines in Solikamsk, 25 km further north. Anticipating its potential, the pair amassed shares, dissuading anyone who threatened to upstage them. This was not for the faint-hearted. Drawn by such a valuable asset in the region, competitors, including criminal organisations, were lurking. But the duo paid no attention. Two years later, having bought the shares of all and sundry, Rybolovlev reached the summit. Owner of 66 per cent of the company's shares, he became chairman of Uralkali's board of directors.

'It was only then, when I'd understood that I'd really taken control, that I undertook a complete tour of the Uralkali mines: a tour of my dominion in a way. It was impressive,' he recalls. 'I spent three days inspecting everything, visiting everything. I took the full measure of how my life was going to change.' Rybolovlev also had control of 20 per cent of Silvinit, another major producer of Russian potash.

These spoils of war only whetted Rybolovlev's appetite. His ambition was to control the export of Russian potassium. The threats against him were becoming more specific. It mattered little; he dived in head first, creating a powerful company that secured a virtual monopoly on potash exports.

But he had made dangerous enemies. Millions of roubles were at stake during this period of rampant ultra-liberalisation. Men scrambled for Russia's raw resources amid the ruins of the USSR and sudden, unexplained deaths were not unusual. To protect his family Rybolovlev moved home to the shores of Lake Geneva, in Switzerland. One of his companies had a subsidiary in Geneva and the cantonal authorities issued him with a resident's permit.

However, in order to run his business, he had to return regularly to Russia, and it was on a trip back there that he was arrested, accused of murder, and ultimately sent to prison.

CHAPTER 5

TIME IN THE CELL

Sir Alfred Hitchcock, brilliant director of *Vertigo*, *Psycho*, *Rear Window*, and *North by Northwest*, is rightly considered the 'Master of Suspense'. A childhood episode was to form his personality and dramatically change his fate, with confinement and authority later becoming key obsessions in his films. Born in 1899 in the London suburb of Leytonstone, later the birthplace of David Beckham, Hitchcock was sent aged five by his father, William, to the local police station by himself. As punishment for bad behaviour, he had to hand the policeman a note whose contents were unknown to him. After reading it, the officer put young Alfred into a cell for ten minutes, saying to him as he opened the doors: 'That's what we do to naughty boys!' The Englishman who would go on to become a Hollywood icon was traumatised by the event and admits to never having forgotten 'the sound and the solidity' of the closing cell door.

Dmitry Rybolovlev did not spend ten minutes in prison, but eleven months, including his thirtieth birthday, on 22

November 1996. It was a moment that seemed disconnected from reality, 'celebrated' to the tune of the 1970s Eagles hit 'Hotel California' that close friends and relatives had managed to have played on the small screen in his cell, as a gift and token of solidarity.

Rybolovlev swears, however, that imprisonment has left no particular mark on him. He prefers to philosophise on the positive effects, describing it as just one experience among many others.

'It remains the darkest period of my life. Never in my whole life, did I imagine that one day I would end up in prison. For the son of two doctors, born into intellectual circles, it wasn't part of the plan. But I aim to get something out of every setback. And that goes for this ordeal too, even if, of course, I would rather not have spent an entire summer in jail in the burning heat, surrounded by prisoners,'[30] he says, opening up for the first time about this period in his life.

Stretching his 185cm frame and getting up from his seat, he sometimes punctuates his story with actions in order to better explain certain situations, but also with disarmingly frank laughter. Perhaps a kind of exorcism? His time in prison will inevitably have marked him. Dmitry Chechkin, public relations director at Uralkali, executive board member for ten years, and later vice president at AS Monaco, recalls a scene that has remained firmly in his mind.

---

30   Interview with the author.

'The only time I saw him cry was at his mother's birthday, while she was talking about his time in prison,' he confides. 'Behind bars, he felt especially bad for his parents, considering the education they had given him and knowing how closely he resembles them: he has the intellect of his father and the energy of his mother.'[31]

In spite of Rybolovlev's enforced confinement, Chechkin continues to believe that 'an angel' watches over him. 'His life has been marked with dangerous and difficult situations,' says Chechkin of his friend.

> He wasn't prepared for prison. When he was locked up, someone offered to buy Uralkali, in exchange for his freedom. It was pure blackmail, but he refused, aware that it wasn't the right thing to do. He preferred to endure months in detention rather than give in. Dmitry Rybolovlev is impervious to pressure; it's one of his strongest character traits. Most men in such a situation would have cracked or would even have been eliminated. But not him. It's a kind of simultaneous courage and thoughtlessness. That's why I believe in his angel.

Rybolovlev had been living in Switzerland for only a few months when he was arrested. He had chosen to exile himself as he knew he was under serious threat. Whenever he went to the Uralkali headquarters at Berezniki, he was accompanied

---

31   Interview with the author.

by bodyguards and travelled from Perm in an armoured car, wearing a bulletproof vest. The sudden financial prosperity of this 'Potassium Tsar' had aroused keen interest in 'raiders', rarely the first people to negotiate according to the rules.

But the danger not only came from assassins. His efforts to free himself from the International Potash Company (IPC), the Russian–Belarussian trading company that had a grip on exports, had made enemies of a different sort. Prior to Rybolovlev taking control of Uralkali the company, together with other firms, had set up IPC to coordinate exports. Now Rybolovlev felt Uralkali was strong enough to negotiate its own export contracts, which meant extricating itself from IPC.

In May 1996, Uralkali shareholders backed his attempt to end the relationship with IPC. Less than a week later, Rybolovlev had barely touched down at Perm, when he was apprehended by police officers.

The accusation was extremely serious. Oleg Lomakin, a local mafia baron nicknamed Prokop, had been arrested on suspicion of murdering Evgeny Panteleymonov, CEO of Neftekhimik, a chemical company based in Perm. Panteleymonov was gunned down in cold blood on 4 September 1995 at the door to his apartment building.

Rybolovlev had relatively recently taken 40 per cent of the shares of Neftekhimik and was chairman of the company's board of directors. Lomakin admitted involvement in the assassination, but told police the killing had been ordered by Rybolovlev and Shevtsov in exchange for $200,000 and two pistols. Lomakin's accusation, thought to be made as part of a plea bargain, put Rybolovlev and his associate behind bars.

Rybolovlev was initially interrogated at the police station, before being moved to a detention centre to await trial. The initial first few days of confinement were particularly difficult. He was bombarded with questions for hours and urged to confess that he had killed Evgeny Panteleymonov. Interrogation methods in Russia are less regulated than in Western Europe and Rybolovlev was far from his usual confident self during the interrogations, with police recording statements day and night to wear down his mental health. He was forced to watch scenes from movies, ones chosen to make a prisoner anxious, perhaps Russian equivalents to the violent scenes in *Midnight Express*.

Among the worst aspects was the uncertainty. In the dead of night, prison guards would arrive and choose someone from the cell. As was likely intended, Rybolovlev's mind wandered, and he imagined the guards hitting the chosen person until he admitted to having committed the crime he'd been arrested for. Every night, long cries and groans would break the silence. Rybolovlev wondered whether he would be next on the guards' list. Broken sleep is not a restorative. The fatigue was extreme. And that was only the beginning.

While waiting for the trial, he came to understand that his provisional detention was to continue, and that life in prison was to become normal. He was dressed in convict clothing and his hair was cut short. One Friday he was thrown into a cell and had to stay there over the weekend with a dozen inmates, in a tiny space.

'There was only a very small window. We had difficulty breathing through the bars of the cell window. It was summer – not far off a heatwave – and there wasn't enough air. One person, in poor health, died in the first twenty-four hours,' Rybolovlev says, recalling the painful moment.

I approached the guards and told them I couldn't stay here because I was at risk of dying. 'And if I die, you will have so many problems,' I added. I was accompanied to the basement and placed in another cold, damp cell. There were four of us.

After a week, I had hoped to be freed – I had even prepared my bag, just in case. I didn't know what was going to happen to me. I had no access to information, and for six long weeks, I was continually transferred from cell to cell. And, each time I hoped to be freed, I was disappointed. I began to fear I was going to be locked up for ten years.

Rybolovlev regularly changed cells, but he will never forget the moment he entered a room where sixty people lived packed together, with three levels of bunk beds. It was a dimly lit space, dirty and poorly maintained, where the suffocating damp made breathing difficult. It was so hot that beads of condensation formed on the cracked ceiling and dripped onto the floor, while the prisoners wore only their underclothes in the stifling heat. In the middle of the room, there was a small table to put their food bowl on and wooden stumps to sit on. But not everyone had the right to sit down.

Like every hermetic environment, prisons have their own codes of behaviour, with rules that it pays to respect. In jail, not everyone is equal. Animal instincts prevail and are necessary for survival. The most powerful inmates form the most important clan. They are the chosen ones: depending on how long they've been in captivity, their criminal history, their contacts, the size of their biceps, or their tattoos. They have the power to sit at the table and dictate the law, to decide who can join them and who can speak. The hierarchy is precise and rigid. It does not shift. Such an environment can easily grind you up.

Rybolovlev carefully assessed the situation. He knew that being a company CEO on the outside was of no value between these walls. In prison, it was his medical studies and diploma in cardiology that would save him. He therefore cautiously introduced himself as simply a doctor and was able to gain the trust of the other inmates. He gave them advice when they showed him their drugs, thrown in a plastic bag and sent by their families – antibiotics they didn't know how to use. Sometimes he even treated prisoners.

'You can be at the top of any game; it doesn't give you any guarantees in prison,' he says. 'Prison forces you to be humble. I tried to understand how the internal rules worked; it's vital to adapt. You can no longer control everything. I thought of it as an experience.'

Behind bars, he rubbed shoulders with people from all walks of life – a mix of different types and different origins. He lived alongside recidivist murderers and young thugs. Very few white-collar criminals are incarcerated in Perm. While waiting to appear before the court for trial and discover the length of his sentence, Rybolovlev kept watching, protecting himself as much as he could, rarely making friends, and communicating as little as possible.

I got used to the idea that this prison was now my home, that I lived there. I processed the rules – I had to identify the boss of the cell then make him an ally. Those that held the power asked simple questions: 'What are you accused of?' and 'Who are you?' That's why at the beginning, I pretended to be a doctor and not a businessman … On the fifth day, once I had analysed the habits and deciphered the profiles of my companions, I told the truth.

Meanwhile, weeks passed, and there was still no progress in the investigation. Because of the heart problems that dated back to his childhood, Rybolovlev managed to get a bed near the only window, thus gaining a little welcome fresh air. As he had done in his business dealings, he studied the key people so that he could better manage the situation. Each time his cell was changed, he would try to become close to the new cell's most respected inmate. He finally found refuge in a more 'welcoming' cell, even though it was one where he was still flanked by about twenty people. Quickly, he disappeared into the background.

'When you are accepted by the most important clan, the one that holds the power, all problems of safety and of daily life disappear. Life doesn't become easier, but more bearable – as long as you obey the rules, obviously,' he says.

But being respected by your cellmates is not a blank cheque. Although Rybolovlev helped his companions deal with illness, he couldn't escape his own health problems. Without the other prisoners knowing, he was checked just once a week and even then the medical check took only a few seconds. He was suffering from a vitamin deficiency and experienced stabbing stomach pains. Luckily, he didn't have toothache, as appointments with the dentist needed to be made months in advance.

In prison, compassion and hygiene are not values shared by everyone. Whenever he could, he would give antibiotics to those inmates who were particularly suffering because of their teeth. It was a question of easing their distress, even if only momentarily. When it was his turn to endure terrible pain in his kidneys, Rybolovlev was puzzled. He had learned to manage on his own, but this time, it was unbearable. The reason: kidney stones. In instances of insufficient hydration, crystals as hard as stone can form in the kidneys and spread through the urinary tract. In his case, the urethra was obstructed, increasing the intensity of pain from his lower back to the stomach and causing renal colic.

'It was extremely difficult to bear. A vital organ was affected, and, poorly treated, could have been even more dangerous, leading to renal failure,' he explains.

The prison staff thought I was pretending: that I was faking the pain in order to be transferred. I demanded that tests be carried out, and with the help of my lawyers, managed to obtain a medical examination. Under close surveillance, I was driven to Perm hospital in a convoy – the same hospital I had worked at as an intern.

I was finally taken care of and given the correct medication. It was an awful time. I was already weakened by three serious infections. My tonsils were swollen and inflamed, and I had a terrible sore throat. It was truly a nightmare.

A small measure of solace came on his thirtieth birthday. Friends and family managed to have the long (six-and-a-half minutes with a third of that the cult guitar solo) 'Hotel California' by The Eagles played on the televised evening programme, in three or four segments.

'It's not my favourite song, but it made me happy,' Rybolovlev says. His loyal supporters also managed to get some subtitles included that said: 'We wish you a happy birthday. And we hope you'll soon be out.'

It was to be his only link with the outside world, as throughout his whole captivity, he didn't receive a single visit. For safety reasons, he had refused to allow his parents and wife to visit him. But also he feared he wouldn't be able to contain his emotions when seeing his father and mother in the visiting room. However, he did catch a glimpse of them when he was summoned to court, after his lawyers had managed to gain a hearing.

'It was a choice to cut myself off from the world. I wanted to leave the outside world to one side,' he says. Rather than feeling sorry for himself, Rybolovlev instead recounts a brief moment of levity, when a defence lawyer handed a letter to a prisoner's wife that was destined for his lover, and vice versa. 'The lawyer mixed them up. On the same day, the prisoner lost his wife and his mistress. But,' Rybolovlev smiles, 'a few weeks later, his wife came back to him.'

This period in jail attracted unwanted media attention, something Rybolovlev tries to avoid. A journalist at the local newspaper, the *Perm News*, from 1990–2013, and editor-in-chief for five of those years, Andrey Nikitin had been following the twists and turns of the case with interest.

'Until he was imprisoned, Dmitry Rybolovlev was undoubtedly a well-known figure in the region, but reports and discussion about him were always moderate. After that, however, his fate was no longer only talked about in the business pages,' Nikitin says.

What happened changed things dramatically. I had met him for the first time in 1992, when he started to invest in Uralkali. I had been present at the company's public management meetings, which he participated in. But I hadn't interviewed him directly, as even at that time, he didn't give interviews. Despite his discretion, you could tell he was very self-assured, ready to face criticism. He had a strong inner confidence. He knew exactly what he wanted, and he was determined to get it.

At the time of his incarceration, our newspaper was very responsive. Rumours claimed that he was in prison because he hadn't wanted to give up his shares in Uralkali in exchange for his freedom, and that, for as long as he held out, he would stay there. It wasn't easy sorting out true from false.

In any case, while in jail, he shared his day-to-day life with real criminals. And even under pressure, he didn't waver. In spite of the impatience he must have felt because the court didn't settle the matter, he did all he could not to draw attention to himself.[32]

During the eleven months of his imprisonment, one of those who Rybolovlev relied on for support was Vadim Vasilyev. The current vice president of AS Monaco looked after Rybolovlev's family in Switzerland, where he himself was living at the time. The two men had not known each other for long, having only met during a conference in Chicago in 1995. Ex-diplomat Vasilyev was at that time vice president of the American company Transammonia, a specialist in fertiliser

---

32 Interview with the author.

trading. Rybolovlev noticed his skill at negotiating and, during a partnership project, hired him to work for Uralkali, later entrusting him with its international subsidiary, as head of exports.

'I have known Dmitry in good times and bad. He's a true friend. When he was in prison, I wasn't able to help him. I couldn't do anything for him directly, but I stayed close to his family,' said Vasilyev. 'We have a trust-based relationship, the two of us.'[33]

In April 1997, Rybolovlev was freed. Eleven months of captivity and suffering came to an end when the Supreme Court acquitted him due to lack of evidence and cleared his name. Sole witness Oleg Lomakin's credibility fell apart after he withdrew his testimony and when two of his henchmen admitted that they had killed Evgeny Panteleymonov. They said they had gunned him down at Lomakin's instigation, something that Lomakin had previously denied before the court. All three men were sentenced to fifteen years' imprisonment.

But perhaps the true mastermind behind the murder has never been formally identified. Against the backdrop of a struggle for control of potassium in Russia, was the whole situation orchestrated by some rival who was eager to get his hands on Uralkali? Rybolovlev, usually so frank, refuses to comment. Other Russian billionaires have experienced run-ins with the Russian judicial system, but few have ever gone

---

33   Interview with the author.

to jail. As one of Rybolovlev's friends insists: 'Believe me, if he was a real oligarch, he would have used his connections and avoided prison.'[34]

The most striking exception of oligarchs who have not been jailed is Mikhail Khodorkovsky, who, during the time he was director of petrol group Yukos, which controlled two per cent of world oil production, was the richest man in Russia. He was finally pardoned by President Vladimir Putin in December 2013, after spending ten years in a Siberian prison camp. In December 2015, however, Russia issued an international warrant for his arrest.[35]

In Pierre Lorrain's view, the Rybolovlev case is different.

'If we are to define oligarchy as being close to the government, then that has never been the case for Rybolovlev. He has always kept his distance from Moscow, with his fiefdom being Perm, where he was imprisoned,' explains the journalist, writer and expert on Russia, where he was a foreign correspondent from 1992 to 2001.

He was accused of murder and in the end, the true instigator and executors of the murder were sentenced. His name was totally cleared. I don't know if Dmitry Rybolovlev is a

---

34 Interview with the author.
35 Arrested in 2003, Khodorkovsky was convicted in 2005 and 2010 on charges of tax evasion, fraud, oil theft, and money laundering, accusations he has always vigorously denied. Not long before his arrest, and like other oligarchs, he had funded liberal political parties, investing millions into support programmes for civil society, campaigning for the construction of private oil pipelines, and opposing the tax on oil companies.

perfectly honest man. Like all those who made their fortunes at the beginning of the 1990s, he seized every possible opportunity, even if what he was doing was barely legal. He functioned at the limits of legality, but without actually infringing it, unlike many oligarchs, who took no notice of the law. The fact remains that in his case the justice system did its job correctly in freeing him. Certainly, during the collapse of the USSR and the ensuing wild shift to privatisation, where everyone was free to invest in private equity, he made his fortune in a cavalier manner, taking advantage of inflation and juggling the rouble with the dollar. But bankers and certain industries such as gas did the same at the time.

While Rybolovlev took advantage of the system to become the majority shareholder of Uralkali, if we look at his background and business behaviour, it doesn't look as if he's the kind of person to hire a hitman. In any case, seen from France, everything Russian is inevitably suspect. It's almost a form of paranoia, when in fact most Russian businessmen are above board. When we talk about the mafia, we associate it with Al Capone. Over there, they think of Bernard Tapie![36] The idea and meaning of mafia are different.[37]

Rybolovlev has chosen to retain the 'formative' aspect of his

---

36 Tapie was chairman of Marseille from 1986 to 1994 when the club won several French titles and the Champions League. Marseille were discovered to have bribed opposing teams in 1993 and Tapie was given a two-year jail sentence for match-fixing and fraud.

37 Interview with the author.

time spent in jail. 'Until then, I only focused on business. Only financial transactions interested me,' he says. 'I had no life experience. Along the way, I have probably made some mistakes. They might well have been the cause of my problems. During those eleven months, I learned a lot about human nature. It was certainly radical, but, somehow, it was useful.'

With a tremor in his voice, he relates the moment he was set free and when, exhausted but relieved, he returned home.

My first reaction was to wonder if I was really free. Until it has really taken place, the doubt wears away at you. So I wasn't able to express my happiness until I was truly on the outside. At the end of the day, once all the formalities were complete, I said to the guard who opened the door for me: 'See you next time!' He was surprised by me saying that, just as I was leaving. So he said to me: 'You're crazy! Go on, get out of here.'

At home, first I stayed in the bathroom for a long time. I let the hot water run over me and I stretched out in the bath: it had been such a long time! It was also a way of cleansing myself of the prison. Then, when it came time to eat, I was surprised to find a fork in my hand. In the cell, we only ate with a spoon. Forks are forbidden: too dangerous! Cutlery can be used as a weapon or to commit suicide.

With a laugh, his cousin Andrey Konogorov, former board member of Uralkali and now in charge of running the private family island of Skorpios, summarises in one sentence the time Rybolovlev spent in prison: 'It was the best university he could have gone to.'[38] But he adds that jail encouraged Rybolovlev to evolve. 'In a way, it helped him to better understand people and the way they work. This enforced stay certainly momentarily held him back, but it allowed him to focus on what matters and to think differently about things.'

Konogorov also describes another, more profound change resulting from the cells in Perm:

Although he was from an Orthodox background, he wasn't particularly interested in religion. But soon after his release from prison, he went to church to be baptised. He then confided to one of his friends: 'If you had been in the cells in my place and went through what I have been through, believe me, you would ask to be baptised immediately.' Since leaving prison, he has become more concerned with religion. Moreover, he has funded the renovation of a church in Berezniki and has contributed, among other things, to the construction of a large episcopal church in the region of Perm, for which he bought some beautiful icons.

When I asked Rybolovlev if prison had taught him some lessons he could apply to the business world, such as staying strong under pressure, his true nature came to the fore. 'I

---

38   Interview with the author.

already had that trait before. And it was very useful to me in prison. I had decided that if I had to stay locked up for ten years, well then, I would do it. But I would never give in to pressure. That has become a kind of life philosophy for me.'

Declared innocent and freed, he quickly regained his ambition. While his wife and daughter remained in Geneva, Rybolovlev regularly travelled the well-worn route between Perm and Berezniki. The journey is one that can now be made in two hours. But back then, accompanied by his loyal companions and bodyguards, it took Rybolovlev five hours and involved travelling through the forest and passing police checkpoints. The road was unpaved and there were no bridges, which meant that Rybolovlev and his companions had to take the ferry. They also had to cope with winter temperatures well below freezing, which made the roads icy. It was hardly a case of them travelling in style. They originally drove a Zhiguli, a popular Russian-made car based on the Fiat 124 and better known in the West under the brand name of Lada.

Despite such long journeys and the endless days spent in Berezniki, Rybolovlev retains fond memories of this period. 'Uralkali is still my baby. It represents an important period in my life. I grew up with it, even if I no longer have any connection with the company.'

Andrey Konogorov travelled between Perm and Berezniki so often with his cousin that he knows every inch of the route by heart. 'I'd get home at the weekend and Dmitry, in the early days, would also spend a lot of time on site,' says this former mechanical engineer who worked for eight years in Siberia before Rybolovlev asked him to join him.

> Little by little, he changed the management; he brought in his confidantes who had also grown up in Perm. We were young, without much experience. This new life was very exciting. It was as though we were in a film, because it was also dangerous: Dmitry, who was protecting his business, always had armed bodyguards to protect him from those who wanted to try to take over Uralkali by abducting or threatening him. On the business side of things, although the company was mainly selling its potassium in Russia, Dmitry actively developed the international market and modified the transport conditions. He senses things, anticipates them. To continue to expand, he had keenly observed the market and the way the Canadians were working at the Potash Corporation of Saskatchewan, the world leaders. He signed partnership agreements with them and other companies. But he had also wanted to build his own empire.

With Rybolovlev in control, the pace of production accelerated. So too did exports, to China, India, Brazil, Germany, and the United States. He diversified, with the production of magnesium salt. In 2001, a terminal in the Baltic Sea was inaugurated in St Petersburg. Four years later, Uralkali acquired 50 per cent of one of its competitors, the Belarusian Potash Company (BPC). Rybolovlev was not afraid either of pressurising the Chinese government, one of his clients, to increase the price of his potassium. By sticking to his guns, he eventually won China over.

In Berezniki, Andrey Konogorov's nights were increasingly short. But he never complained. 'At any rate, there wasn't much else to do there except work,' confides the man who was to end up on the management committee of Uralkali.

I love hunting and fishing but I didn't often have the opportunity to do either. To relax, we played a bit of tennis and volleyball, a sport that Dmitry sometimes played with us. Then we went and had a sauna after our games. I was sleeping at a hotel and would be at the office by eight in the morning. Dmitry would call me at any time, often after dinner, to get all the news. And there was no way I'd tell him that I didn't have time, or that I was too exhausted to answer him. After a forty-minute chat, it was impossible to get to sleep.

You must understand: he put all of his energy into Uralkali, blood, sweat, and tears, twenty-four hours a day so that that company would grow, despite all obstacles. He studied all the markets, was attentive to crises, and left nothing to chance. Production increased considerably and when the prices were at their peak, he could've sold everything. He had the opportunity to. It was tempting, but he preferred sticking it out and taking a long-term view.

Dmitry Rybolovlev is an uncompromising boss, who ensures

that everyone falls into line. When people don't immediately comply, he can reveal his curt or even aggressive side. This is borne out by a Russian investigative journalist, who collected off-the-record statements from former employees.

'They were terrified. And not just the workers! Vladislav Baumgertner, the managing director, also feared his short temper. He was often lectured on the phone when something wasn't going well or came out in the press,' claimed one anonymous source. 'From Switzerland, where he was living, he easily reprimanded the leaders, even those who hadn't done anything. I don't know whether he threatened everyone in this way, or if everyone was as impressionable as Baumgertner.'[39]

Yuri Bogdanov doesn't fall into this category. The Moscow native was working as an auditor – for the Arthur Andersen agency and Ernst & Young – when he was approached by Uralkali. At just twenty-four years of age, he became the company's financial controller, looking after the accounts.

'I agreed to the position because Uralkali had a very young leadership: the managing director was only thirty-one, for instance. You could sense the ambition, the enthusiasm, and also a deliberate policy of conquest,' he notes.

And also, while we were all Russian, we also had noticeably similar backgrounds, so much so that a refreshing Western spirit governed our team. Dmitry Rybolovlev is an exacting, highly attentive boss, who sets high goals and does everything to attain them. He also accepts his responsibilities and recognises when he's at fault.[40]

As Uralkali grew, Rybolovlev decided, in 2006, to list it on the London Stock Exchange. The company now claimed 10 per cent of the global market in potash-based fertiliser, with turnover up by 77 per cent in relation to the 2004 figures. Rybolovlev was considering listing around 20 per cent of the company's shares.

Working with him was Yuri Bogdanov, now financial director of the family office, Rigmora Holdings Limited, in Monaco. There, in functional offices on Avenue Princesse-Grace, opposite the sea and the Larvotto beaches, Bogdnaov oversees some thirty staff, mostly young and of various nationalities, who handle the affairs of the Rybolovlev family. A true-blue financier, this very Cartesian and loyal employee appreciates the intuition that guides Rybolovlev and makes him so unpredictable.

He's not a card player or someone who throws the die and just lets it fall. He makes bets, but they're informed bets, even if that is surprising and even extraordinary the first time you witness it.

I remember when we worked on the listing. Everything was ready to be taken to market; we were on the starting blocks. There were just twenty-four hours remaining before the launch. He went to London, on a kind of promotional tour to feel out the way the market was going to react. His perception was that the signs were bad, that the company was not going to be estimated at the level it deserved. At the last moment, in spite of the work undertaken up until then, he cancelled everything. He was right.

Rybolovlev shared his disappointment in a statement: 'Given the attractive fundamentals in the sector, the high potential growth, and the solid financial situation of the company, I estimate that the market has not recognised Uralkali at its rightful value.'

Several weeks later, Bogdanov was to look on, stunned and powerless, at the disaster that was to strike Uralkali: a disaster that threatened to bring about the fall of Dmitry Rybolovlev.

CHAPTER 6

URALKALI: A FORTUNE DISSOLVED AND REMADE

The last three mayors of Berezniki, a town with 150,000 inhabitants, have all been former employees of Uralkali. That fact illustrates the influence this producer of mineral fertiliser, particularly potash and potassium chloride, has had on the town. Installed in his vast office on the third floor of the town hall, overlooking the main square, Sergey Petrovic Dyakov has sat in the mayoral chair since 2009. He is also a delegate to the regional parliament. Born in Perm in 1956, he began working in the Uralkali mines in 1978 as an electrician, and rose from supervisor to chief engineer to head of mining at his terminal, until he was appointed director in 2000. He could almost be considered the company's historian – a company that received a real burst of energy when Rybolovlev arrived on the scene.

'Because of the privatisations and the possibility for workers to receive shares based on the number of years they had worked there, there were a great many shareholders. Then, when Dmitry Rybolovlev took over, Uralkali changed. He reorganised everything, particularly at a commercial level and for product sales,' recalls Dyakov.

> He set us off along capitalist lines. I am also grateful for the fact that he retained most of the technical staff, while also promoting their value. Within a few years, we had started exporting our production and had become the world's third largest potassium company. In 2006, there were 16,000 employees. The organisation was at its best, everyone was optimistic, management was efficient, and sales were continuously growing. Uralkali was a great brand and of an international standard. We were expanding rapidly and had impressive potassium reserves. And then the incident occurred.[41]

This is a masterpiece of understatement. In October 2006, for still unknown reasons, thousands of litres of water poured into the No. 1 mine. Gigantic holes formed, the earth shook, and the potassium chloride extracted from salt was flooded. Some 450 workers were trapped at the bottom of the mine, becoming increasingly afraid as the walls and pillars of salt supporting underground ceilings began to dissolve. Radio contact was lost. It became impossible to stop the flow of water. For ten days, all hands were on deck to try to save

---

41   Interview with the author.

Uralkali and the workers. As the region held its breath, engineers frantically struggled to do what they could, mainly using devices intended for pumping sea water.

'Imagine putting a sugar cube in a cup of tea,' said the chief land surveyor at Uralkali. 'Well, that is what happened at Berezniki.'

A giant crater formed and led to the closure of the oldest mine. Rybolovlev learned of the situation from his CEO. He was at home in Switzerland and arrived at the mine the next day. 'The accident is a difficult memory for me,' Rybolovlev says.

> Once I got there, I listened to the experts and went down into the mine to assess the damage. I made the decision to evacuate the workers in the middle of the night. Day and night we tried to find solutions. We had to save the mines, of course, but we particularly wanted to avoid any deaths. It was extremely tense. I was really only able to breathe again once the last man had been brought out.[42]

That there was no loss of life was the only positive outcome. The negatives, however, were huge, severely hampering economic growth and causing an ecological disaster. Fifty million tonnes of potassium had gone for ever and several million euros worth of equipment had been lost underground. Power stations had been damaged.

---

42   Interview with the author.

While Rybolovlev was relieved that no one had been seriously injured, the catastrophe made him lose both his money and his illusions. Uralkali's value wasted away, literally. Only a few weeks earlier, the company had been set to be listed on the London Stock Exchange.

'That was a sad coincidence. I can't imagine what would have happened to Uralkali if we had joined the stock exchange as intended,' sighs Yuri Bogdanov. 'At the time, because of the flood, we lost several tens of millions. We abandoned a large mine, as well as equipment. But, fortunately, everybody was safe and sound.'

Mayor Dyakov, technical director at Uralkali at the time, talks of 'a situation of crisis and stress, during which Rybolovlev demonstrated force of character'.

For example, going down into the mine at five o'clock in the morning once everyone had been evacuated. He didn't go into a spin, never panicked, and settled things without hesitation. He trusted the staff and made the necessary decisions. Coordination between local government and scientists at Uralkali was harmonious. It wasn't easy, because we had never experienced an ordeal such as this.

Exacerbating the situation the mines were not, as is usually the case, sited outside town, but in the heart of it, which caused many people to flee and sparked chaos. After the incident, the mine was a ruin. Some people found themselves out of work, while others did not try to hide their fury. The government set up an inquiry which concluded that the disaster had been an 'inevitable natural catastrophe', a geological rather than technical incident.

More than a decade on, the landscape remains devastated by the subsidence caused by the infiltration of water into the mines. Rybolovlev has funded the construction of nurseries and a primary school in Berezniki, as well as a hospital, which opened in 2010. The inscriptions on the façades of these establishments reveal that Uralkali financed them.

Uralkali had to be restored, but Rybolovlev rose to the challenge. He modernised infrastructure, invested in the mines whose potential he continued to believe in, and built a new power station. Production soared again.

'It was simple: his aim was to be the top potassium producer in the world. Being second doesn't interest him,' summarises Mayor Dyakov. Though the first mine had vanished from Uralkali's map, four others remained to help Rybolovlev achieve his dreams of conquest. In October 2007, less than one year after the collapse of the mine, the company made a second, and more successful attempt to list in London.

'Dmitry is not just a manager, he's a strategist,' enthuses Andrey Konogorov, his cousin, who was at Rybolovlev's side in Berezniki.

Because frankly, in the early 1990s, who outside of Russia would have bet on Uralkali? The company in its form at the time was not particularly well established, and the market was dominated by longer-standing businesses. Not many would have bet on Uralkali then, besides him. And that is his strength: having vision.[43]

'Part of it is instinct, but mostly it's having real business sense,' adds Yuri Bogdanov.

The introduction of 12.5 per cent of Uralkali's capital to the London Stock Exchange, compared to the 10 per cent initially envisaged, was one of the year's success stories. The order book for shares exploded – there was twenty-five times more demand than stock for sale. The potash market reached unseen heights, so much so that Uralkali's share price surged 300 per cent in only eight months, bringing the value of the 12.5 per cent of shares to $948 million. The company's shares were also listed on the Moscow Stock Exchange.

'Its success owed much to him. Dmitry Rybolovlev is pragmatic and not afraid of making decisions, particularly during times of crisis, and especially when the decision is contrary to the opinion of others. He is a perfectionist who wants the best. He's a sponge, absorbing every last piece of information,' insists Alexey Kosarev, ex-officer and head of security at Uralkali. Kosarev, who now lives in Moscow after having followed his boss to Monaco for three years, adds:

---

43   Interview with the author.

It was the right moment for him to launch the IPO [initial public offering, the first time the stock of a private company is offered for sale to the public], as one year earlier, he had felt that he needed to postpone it. He is open to discussion, listens to opposing points of view, but he's the one that decides. All in all, he's a true capitalist.

With a 66 per cent share, Dmitry Rybolovlev was a rich man, very rich. And all thanks to a chemical element necessary for the production of agricultural fertilisers. For the first time, he entered the list of 100 largest fortunes established by the American magazine *Forbes*. Shrewdly, he diversified his portfolio, investing, for example, in the biotechnology sector via a Swiss company.

In the Uralkali saga, there is no shortage of twists and turns. Especially when new characters arrive. It's time to introduce Igor Sechin, a figure close to Russian President Vladimir Putin, who was chief of staff when Putin was first Deputy Mayor of St Petersburg. Sechin's influence grew when Putin was elected President for the first time in March 2000. That is why Sechin now presides over the board of directors of oil group Rosneft, which made a net profit of €900 million in the first three months of 2014 on a turnover of $20 billion. In May 2008, Sechin was also Deputy Prime Minister of the Russian Federation.

Although the first investigation had concluded that the flooding at the mine had been an accident, Sechin ordered a second inquiry, led by the Federal Environmental, Engineering, and Nuclear Inspection Service. In November 2008, this inquiry concluded that negligence had occurred and that the flooding could have been prevented. Rybolovlev was ordered to pay for the damage. The total sum was not established, but some estimates put it at around €1 billion. Uralkali's share price on the London Stock Exchange plummeted.

As he is not the type to buckle under pressure, Rybolovlev only agreed to pay for part of the infrastructure loss. It was not enough. The pressure from above became constant. Respected American journalist John Helmer, former professor in political science and living in Moscow as a foreign correspondent since 1989, outlined a hypothesis on his 'Dances with Bears' blog:

> Hints from Prime Minister Vladimir Putin, Sechin, and others suggests they have in mind to dispose of Rybolovlev, and reorganise Uralkali under the control of Viatcheslav Kantor, who currently controls the nitrogen fertiliser producer and exporter, Acron.[44]

An oligarch, Viatcheslav Moshe Kantor was also president of the Russian Jewish Congress and is still president of the

---

44   Dances with Bears; 'In Bad Odour – Russian Government Plays Fertilizer Games, While China Suffers Farmland Drought', blog entry by John Helmer, 16 February 2009, http://johnhelmer.net/?p=774.

European Jewish Congress. Just as Rybolovlev once did, he lives in Cologny, the upmarket Geneva suburb.

Rybolovlev tried to steer as far away from politics as possible, even if he was happy to take advantage of the protection offered by Yury Trutnev, former Mayor, then Governor of Perm, and Minister of Natural Resources and the Environment from 2004 to 2012. Trutnev is now the Deputy Prime Minister and Presidential Envoy to the Far Eastern Federal District. He had taken the view that, as there was no precedent, it was difficult to establish Uralkali's liability. For him a geological incident had most likely caused the subsidence and flooding of mine no. 1.

Rybolovlev was now locked in an unequal struggle against Sechin and the muscle of the Kremlin. To make matters worse, problems had emerged on the domestic front; he was going through a difficult divorce process that seemed to drag on for ever. Backed into a corner, Rybolovlev chose to act cautiously. In June 2010, he sold 53.2 per cent of Uralkali's capital to three businessmen close to the Kremlin. Reluctantly? Let's just say he was strongly encouraged to sell and that the sale conditions were very respectable.

Billionaire Suleyman Kerimov, representative for the Republic of Dagestan at the Russian Council of the Federation, took 25 per cent of Uralkali. In football, Kerimov is best known for his period as president of his hometown club FK Anzhi Makhachkala, where he brought in players such as Roberto Carlos and Samuel Eto'o, paying the latter €20 million a year. In Monaco he is better known for having lost control of his Ferrari on the Promenade des Anglais in Nice (both he and his TV presenter passenger ended up in hospital with burns). Filaret Galchev, who made his fortune in cement and coal trading, obtained 15 per cent of Uralkali; Alexander Nesis, head of the ICT Group specialising in precious metals, received 13.2 per cent. The three partners were granted a loan of $3 billion by VTB (Vneshtorgbank), a bank wholly owned by the state since 2007. This triggered a hypothesis that Kerimov was a figurehead, acting on behalf of others close to a government that was eager to recover the near-totality of potassium-producing companies.

Author of *The Mysterious Rise of Vladimir Putin* and *Moscou et la naissance d'une nation* (*Moscow and the Birth of a Nation*), Pierre Lorrain elaborates:

> Rybolovlev controlled one of the economic activities that the Kremlin considered strategic, that is, potash and chemical fertiliser. It became so important that a few years after getting out of prison, he was politely asked to step aside from Uralkali, receiving a very large pay-out. He sold most of his shares and was intelligent enough to move overseas, without making a fuss and never getting involved in politics. Most entrepreneurs who engaged in Kremlin politics under Boris Yeltsin confirmed their allegiance to Vladimir Putin, who, after summoning them, warned 'the state will not interfere in your business as long as you do not interfere in politics, and as long as you pay your taxes'.

This was how, in the summer of 2008, a year and a half after Putin had rejected his initial offer, Roman Abramovich's resignation as governor of the province of Chukotka was accepted. When Dmitry Medvedev became President, with Putin as Prime Minister, Medvedev allowed Abramovich to step down as governor of the autonomous district in the cold regions of far-west Russia – larger than France (but with only 53,000 inhabitants) and rich in minerals. The Chelsea owner had been elected eight years earlier, winning more than 90 per cent of the vote. He spent billions of roubles on the region – a region which he modernised and whose GDP he doubled.[45]

Although he had quit the potassium business, Dmitry Rybolovlev was not necessarily unhappy. He slipped away from Uralkali while at the top. And he pocketed $6.5 billion by selling his shares – an operation spread across nine months. He also offloaded his shares in Silvinit, the other Russian potassium specialist, then sixth-largest in the world, and which would be taken over by Uralkali at the end of 2010.

For Anna Kupriyanova, a specialist in fertiliser markets and an analyst at Uralsib Capital, Rybolovlev had no cause to complain: 'He earned almost 20 per cent more than what it was worth on the market, a good price given the penalties the mining accident could have incurred.' Not to mention

---

45   Abramovich primarily built his fortune by buying the oil company Sibneft from
      the state for €75 million, along with Boris Berezovsky. Ten years later, he sold his
      share in Sibneft for several billions of euros to the state company Gazprom, the
      largest gas exporter in the world.

that, as part of the sale deal, he received a 10 per cent share in Polyus Gold, the largest producer of gold in Russia.

In any case, with Sechin supervising the energy sector for the government, did Rybolovlev have a choice? Not really, according to Russian expert Pierre Lorrain:

> The atmosphere in the Russian business milieu was espe-cially toxic after the Khodorkovsky affair, the dismantling of Yukos, and purchase of its assets by state companies, in particular Rosneft. It was also the period of 'raiding': where businessmen took advantage of the complicity of judicial, law enforcement, and other state authorities to create entirely fabricated criminal files against competitors,
>
> The victims were then sentenced to prison and their assets were seized by the same legal system that had sold them to them during rigged auctions. These practices are now subject to stricter controls, but from 2005 to 2010 they occurred fre-quently. Also, when high-ranking state personalities advise someone like Rybolovlev (who had already experienced preventive detention) to sell to certain individuals, he had two possibilities: obey and get the best possible price for the transaction, or start a battle he could never win.[46]

In a rapidly expanding market, the rise of Uralkali has continued apace. This ore, the basis of many agricultural

---

46   Interview with the author.

fertilisers, is becoming increasingly sought after as the world's population grows, while the global arable land area remains unchanged. It has been enough to whet appetites, even triggering a diplomatic crisis between Russia and Belarus (which was only resolved after the intervention of Vladimir Putin) as well as changes of ownership and control that have included a Chinese sovereign wealth fund taking a stake in the firm.

By 2014, Uralkali was selling 12 million tonnes of potash. More than 90 per cent of its turnover results from international markets, primarily in Asia and Latin America. Today the group operates five mines and seven production sites in Russia. However, in mid-November 2014, Solikamsk-2, Uralkali's second-largest mine, representing one-fifth of Uralkali's global production, was flooded. In a similar situation to the one which Rybolovlev had to deal with in 2006 (which reminds us how much risk this activity involves), water infiltration in the mine's galleries led to its collapse. Again a crater appeared: this one with a diameter of 20 metres and a depth of 30 metres. As the days passed, and despite attempts to pump and divert the water, the hole continued to grow. While the mine, situated in Solikamsk, 25 km from Berezniki and 180 km from Perm, has an uncertain future, areas of human habitation were, fortunately, barely touched.

Rybolovlev continues to follow the adventures of Uralkali, with a touch of paternalism, but from afar, and without any special emotion. It's not his style. He cut the umbilical cord as soon as the company was sold.

'He transformed Uralkali into an international colossus. He was the kind of president who informed himself about everything and made decisions,' recalls Dmitry Chechkin, who now lives in Portugal but who worked alongside Rybolovlev for seven years.[47] 'Once everything was wrapped up, what was he going to do with his life? What was his next challenge going to be? Where was he going to live and what would he invest in? He spent time asking himself those questions, and he asked us too. He certainly wasn't going to do nothing. He still had so much energy to expend.'

The answer was to be AS Monaco, where Rybolovlev – for whom loyalty is not a hollow word – would appoint Chechkin vice president.

---

47   Interview with the author.

CHAPTER 7

SQUABBLING WITH THE FRENCH FOOTBALL FAMILY

Gstaad, in the Swiss Alps: its 7,000 cows (equal to the number of inhabitants) and its members of the jet set, who go there to hurtle down the ski slopes. Rybolovlev owns luxury chalets in Gstaad, with an estimated value of €120 million. It was in one of these chalets that he spent New Year's Eve in 2012. He had been head of AS Monaco for a year, but not everything was going as intended. The club was well on its way to returning to Ligue 1, but there was still much to do within the club, while relations with the French football family were in need of diplomacy. Among the billionaire's New Year's Eve guests was 47-year-old Vadim Vasilyev, a former graduate of the Moscow State Institute of International Relations and now a diplomat turned businessman, specialising in international negotiations.

Vasilyev was no longer director of exports at Uralkali, the potash giant run by Rybolovlev. Vasilyev had preferred to regain his freedom, investing in the stock exchange, real estate, and the hospitality industry. His professional relationship with Rybolovlev had been transformed into a friendship. The two men often spent holidays together and on one of them, Rybolovlev taught Vasileyev how to surf, on the Hawaiian island of Kauai, a heavenly setting in the Pacific Ocean where Rybolovlev had bought actor Will Smith's villa for €14 million.

As midnight and 2013 approached, Rybolovlev shared his idea with Vasilyev. 'I have a proposition for you,' he said, encouraging him to join AS Monaco.

He needed, at the club, to surround himself with people he trusted and who had experience, even if they weren't from the realm of football. He'd thought long and hard about his choice. He's the kind of person who makes decisions that may seem surprising at first but that turn out to be good ones,

says Vasilyev. 'I didn't think about it for long. He asked me to disengage myself from my activities, assuring me that I had several months to work everything out. A week later, I felt that I really only had a few days to do it.'[48]

In January 2013, having just become the chairman's advisor, Vasilyev attended the Ballon d'Or awards ceremony with Rybolovlev in Zurich. The Ballon d'Or was awarded to

---

48   Interview with the author.

Barcelona's Lionel Messi, with Cristiano Ronaldo from Real Madrid the runner-up and Messi's Barcelona team mate Andrés Iniesta in third place.

'Initially, it was a bit difficult to enter this new world. I was under pressure, with my other business to sort out,' Vasilyev explains.

> In Russia, people say: 'The eyes are scared but the hands do the work.' It's a way of saying that you feel the fear but do the job anyway And then I immediately got caught up in this job that intersects with all the other jobs I've had up until now, combining trade, travel, psychology, relationships with players or organisations, and passion. There were parallels with hospitality: in Moscow, in the 1990s, chefs were fought over and the environment was unstable, meaning you had to constantly adapt. I reproduced this approach in football, trying to understand and get an overview. Otherwise, you can quickly lose your temper and your footing.

He learned very quickly, and the partnership works perfectly. 'We don't call each other every day. He allows me a lot of freedom,' confirms the vice president. 'He is there to validate strategic choices and investments. Although he is very flexible, he keeps an eye on everything. Dmitry knows how to establish priorities and focus on the essentials.'

However, a year as Monaco's owner had already passed; an educative year. As Rybolovlev commented when introducing me to Vasilyev at the American bar of the Hôtel de Paris: 'I learned the hard way.'

'I told him that the hardest thing is to manage the club with your head, not your heart,' reveals Jean-Marc Goiran, a close friend of the royals (Prince Albert is his son's godfather) and the head of Jess Group, which negotiates contracts with sporting personalities.

Lacking knowledge of the milieu, the chairman committed some casting errors with some of the leaders. Football is not a normal and rational business. Rybolovlev is intelligent and has admitted his mistakes, which have cost him dearly. He also believed that buying stars like Falcao – a major attraction at the time, among the strikers – would be enough to win and to fill the stadium. He wanted to go too quickly while having some fun, neglecting, for instance, the importance of an outstanding training centre. The philosophy, since then, has changed. Vadim Vasilyev has really helped. You immediately sense that he's a good person, and highly intelligent. Even if he didn't master football, he knew when to listen and was eager to learn, unlike Jérôme de Bontin,[49] for instance, who had good ideas but who never wanted to be involved in the scene.[50]

---

49 French-American businessman Jérôme de Bontin, close to Prince Albert, presided over AS Monaco from April 2008 to February 2009, where he was also the administrator. Three years later, he became the managing director of the New York Red Bulls, until 2014.

50 Interview with the author.

The rise of Vasilyev proved lightning fast: the chairman's advisor became, in March 2013, sports director. Five months later, in August, Vasilyev became vice president, replacing Jean-Louis Campora, seventy-four, who resigned just eight months after his return as vice president in charge of external affairs.

Dr Campora's previous time at ASM lasted much longer. A well-known figure in the principality, he was at the head of the club from 1975 to 2003. Under his presidency, Monaco won five of its seven league titles, three Coupes de France, and one Coupe de la Ligue. He had regretfully observed, in the pages of *L'Équipe*, how the club had 'brutally broken away from a number of emblematic figures', distancing itself from its roots and history by generating 'a kind of radical break and frustration for the supporters'.

Campora was, however, also a respected vice president of the Ligue de Football Professionnel. So he was brought out of retirement by Rybolovlev for the specific purpose of appeasing the conflict with the LFP, which was growing in intensity. After a decade in relative exile, Campora was happy to return to the club and hoped to put things right.

'Shortly after he became chairman, Rybolovlev did me the courtesy of wishing to make my acquaintance, thinking I would be a good person to meet. We had lunch together for the first time to talk about football in the principality,' explains the man who for ten years also directed the Monegasque National Council, the parliament's sole chamber. 'I answered his questions clearly, even if using interpreters complicates things ... He doesn't see football as an investment but has a genuine passion.'[51]

The two men met twice at the Métropole in Joël Robuchon's double Michelin-starred restaurant, and then at Rybolovlev's home. Rybolovlev asked Campora, via Willy De Bruyn, to work with him. The tax situation needed to be dealt with, in particular the growing resistance of other clubs to the advantages Monaco received through its French players paying reduced income tax and its foreign players none at all – thanks to an order dating back to February 1869.

On 21 March, 2013, the LFP had decided, based on a provision in the Sports Code, to force all clubs to locate their head offices to France as of 1 June 2014. Failure to do so could lead to clubs being expelled. In his missive to the professional clubs, Frédéric Thiriez, the president of the LFP, explained matters.

The situation is not new and we have amply debated it within the League in 2003–2004. So ASM had pledged to recruit a maximum of French players. But the problem has amplified considerably owing to the economic crisis, the fall in TV rights in France, the arrival at the head of Monaco of a shareholder with seemingly unlimited resources and, above all, a recruitment policy 80 per cent reoriented towards foreigners.

The noose was tightening.

---

51 Interview with the author.

Two months later Monaco fought back, filing an appeal before the Council of State. Rybolovlev was inflexible: it was out of the question to transfer the head office of the club (a Monegasque limited company) to France and pay taxes there. The club endeavoured to diffuse the situation through lobbying, seeking to meet the club's top executives, one by one, to convince them of the Monegasque specificity. This was also a chance for Vasilyev to familiarise himself with the leaders of French football. The vice president relied on the people skills of Campora. But not everything went to plan for the ex-boss of ASM.

'Vadim Vasilyev had arrived not long before and our discussions were again complicated owing to the language barrier, which was holding back direct contact with the League,' Campora recalls.

> I was ready to serve the club, but it wasn't easy. The results were mitigated, because I thought I could be more useful than I was. I have no regrets about my return, but I must confess that I didn't contribute a great deal. Since I'd left ASM, many of the other leaders had changed. The climate was tense, the economic crisis was keenly felt, and the clubs dreaded the 75 per cent tax so much that everyone was kind of fed up. I got the feeling that there were ditches to fill in that had not all been filled.

The climax to this 'war of nerves' took place on 3 May 2013, at Nice airport. Anxious to appease the conflict between the LFP and Monaco, and keen to show he was the ultimate boss of French football, Noël Le Graët, President of the French Football Federation, entered the fray. Accompanied by Victoriano Melero, deputy CEO in charge of public and security affairs and head of the president's cabinet, he met Rybolovlev discreetly in an airport lounge. With Rybolovlev were De Bruyn, the club's administrator, and his lawyer for the past six years, Tetiana Bersheda, who handled the translation.

The discussion lasted barely five minutes. Le Graët started by stating that he had nothing against Monaco. Immediately, Rybolovlev, who doesn't beat about the bush or stand on ceremony, replied: 'Let's get straight to the point.'

Le Graët did so. In exchange for Rybolovlev maintaining the head office of his club in the principality, the Federation boss suggested Monaco's owner pay €200 million, spread over five or six years. The compensation, Le Graët said, was calculated on estimates as to the difference in costs of the total payroll in France and in the principality. Rybolovlev was left reeling. Cut to the quick, he snapped his folder shut: 'We've wasted our time, both of us. Thank you and goodbye.' Rybolovlev then got up and left, followed by his lawyer, leaving the Federation's representatives stunned.

Not someone to be dictated to, Rybolovlev hates being presented with a fait accompli. 'There was a misunderstanding,' confirmed De Bruyn. 'The road to hell is paved with good intentions. Noël Le Graët doubtless meant well, but he was clumsy. Rybolovlev doesn't like other people negotiating on his behalf. He was furious.'[52]

Le Graët also felt offended, having flown to Nice for a meeting that lasted just ten minutes. But Polyglot Bersheda defends her boss. The jurist explains:

The meeting with Noël Le Graët was rather cold. Perhaps certain people tried to present themselves as intermediaries. But in any case, they contributed in a negative way because Dmitry Rybolovlev received information that did not correspond at all to the views of the president of the Federation and vice versa.

One trait characterises Rybolovlev: he never gives in under pressure. You can present your arguments to him, your reasoning; explain your logic to him. He is very open-minded and a good listener. But as soon as you try to up the ante, or if he feels the slightest threat, he resists. Using those tactics, there is absolutely no chance of getting anywhere. That's what happened with the '€200 million or nothing'.

You have to understand his position: he became the chairman of a football club out of passion and because he lives in Monaco. He is close to the French culture; his children speak the language fluently even if he himself hasn't totally mastered it. After his arrival, a lot of money was invested into the club, and would turn out to be sunk costs. After recruiting

---

numerous players, he is now being asked to pay €200 million for Monaco to establish its head office in France, whereas that has never been the case since the creation of the club, over ninety years ago.[53]

The meeting also underlined the fact that, whatever intermediaries might say, offer or try to negotiate, there was only one man who made the decisions. Richard Olivier, president of the National Directorate of Management Control (DNCG), the financial watchdog for French clubs, took note of Rybolovlev's strong personality when the Russian presented the ASM accounts in June 2013. 'Mr Rybolovlev is impenetrable and indecipherable. But you can tell that he is the one with the power,' Olivier told *France Football* magazine.

The day after the meeting with Noël Le Graët Monaco lost a home game to Caen, which if they had won it, would have mathematically ensured a return to Ligue 1. Rybolovlev was furious and confirmed in a communiqué on the club's website that he deemed the Federation's requirements 'totally unacceptable'. In short, for him the Federation's demands amounted to little more than racketeering. Anxious to rectify this, the FFF claimed it was ASM that 'had offered to pay €200 million based on a payment schedule and terms and conditions to be defined.'

It is difficult to be certain. Some accuse Campora, Le

Graët's friend, of having been made aware of this amount and of even having negotiated with him, before telling Prince Albert (but not Rybolovlev, who was in Los Angeles) that he had 'negotiated a good agreement'. Campora denies this. 'I had no power for discussion whatsoever. I didn't discuss finances, I contented myself with providing information and communicating with the clubs,' he affirms. 'And Monaco didn't make any proposals with a budget to anyone at all.'

The Minister of Sports, Valérie Fourneyron, got involved in the debate, deploring on RMC [Radio Monte Carlo] 'that AS Monaco immediately threatened legal action as soon as talks began. The FFF and the LFP made the right decision in trying to settle this affair by working together and talking things through.'

The tensions continued, with Campora preferring to give the whole thing a wide berth. 'I decided to end the whole collaboration. Rybolovlev, with his advisors, had taken things in hand,' he confesses.

I'd said it from the start, to avoid pitfalls, a go-between who spoke French and could provide a link between the chairman, the club and the organisations was necessary. Vadim Vasilyev initially sought advice from me to deconstruct the mechanisms of football, then he very quickly became comfortable with all of that. He got hooked.

Vasilyev donned the vice president's suit, vacated by

Campora. He found himself on the frontline and relied on De Bruyn to defend Monaco's strategy before the UCPF, the clubs' union, or before the league's board of directors. They argued, in talks and in a leaflet distributed among footballing leaders, that Monaco's purchase of players such as Falcao and James Rodriguez (deals made easier by the tax concessions) benefited everyone as they made the league more attractive to TV companies and sponsors. Success in Europe would improve the standing of French clubs in UEFA rankings, and the money Monaco spent on buying or loaning players from French clubs would circulate throughout the system.

'This was difficult at first because it was not my role to talk with other leaders, especially since there had been unanimity against us,' summarises Vasilyev. 'During the first meetings with the league, I felt hostile reactions. We also had our shortcomings, since we were sort of living in a vacuum. We didn't get discouraged and presented our project several times. It took time to convince people.'

At this point another potential intermediary appeared. Michel Denisot had been a journalist, TV presenter and commentator, and head of Canal+ Sport. But when meeting him during the 2013 Cannes Film Festival, it was another of Denisot's previous roles, that of president of Paris Saint-Germain, that drew Rybolovlev's attention. Cannes led to more meetings, in Monaco, which led many to believe Denisot was about to assume an official role within ASM – a club he says he wrote to as a child to receive 'flags signed by players of the time'.

Denisot, who is also a vice president of Berrichonne de Châteauroux, his hometown club, appeared to become the chairman's advisor, responsible in particular for institutional issues, filling the void left by Campora's withdrawal. Denisot, with his dry wit, told Rybolovlev that he intended to 'change mindsets', and set up several meetings. Via Denisot, Rybolovlev met on a yacht with Nasser al-Khelaifi, president of Paris Saint-Germain, who was passing through Monaco. A round-table discussion also took place with Vincent Labrune, head of Olympique de Marseille.

This led to a dinner at the renowned Le Cinq restaurant in the Four Seasons Hotel George V, a stone's throw from the Champs-Élysées. The delectable menu boasts shelled spider crab served in its shell (€90), roasted blue lobster (€120), grilled and glazed pigeon with truffle and olives (€95), and iced dark chocolate with *carambar* and grilled peanut crisps (€36). But the main item on the menu was the repairing of relationships after the about-face a few weeks earlier at Nice airport.

To facilitate the meal, Denisot 'sold' Rybolovlev the idea that negotiation was possible and that the authorities were no longer going to take a hardline approach. By text message, he mentioned that Le Graët wished to modify the statutes in exchange for financial aid (which would go towards training young players). He also suggested that should an agreement be reached, Monaco could host a match with the French national team – which would have been a first. In addition, Le Graët insinuated, via Denisot, that he would be willing to sell to ASM the young prodigy from En Avant de Guingamp,[54] midfielder Giannelli Imbula, who had just been voted best player in Ligue 2.

However, by the end of the dinner at Le Cinq, Rybolovlev had made no progress. Denisot hinted at another meeting at the Federation's headquarters. The billionaire asked what type of agreement he might expect, and the journalist, producer, and TV presenter replied that he would find out, but that the amount would remain at €200 million. Needless to say, Rybolovlev never returned to Paris. In mid-July 2013, Imbula joined Marseille, signing a five-year contract for a transfer fee of €7.5 million, plus bonuses.[55] Perhaps feeling awkward about these developments, which were never made public, Noël Le Graët and Michel Denisot[56] did not respond to my requests for an interview.

Previously Denisot told *L'Équipe* of his dealings with Rybolovlev: 'We talked during the Cannes Film Festival 2013. I went to see him in Monaco, and I put him in touch with other club presidents. That was it. Now I just wish him happy birthday by text message.'

---

54   Noël Le Graët was president of Guingamp 1972–1991, then 2002–2011, the year he became president of the FFF. The club is now headed by his son-in-law, Bertrand Desplat.

55   Imbula subsequently moved to Porto, then, in 2016, to Stoke City, by which time his price had more than trebled.

56   The author was unable to interview Noël Le Graët and Michel Denisot .

While no contract had been signed, Denisot sent a hefty €100,000 bill relating to the connections he established for ASM.

'All that for a few lunches and meetings that led to nothing concrete and which the club could just as easily have organised themselves,' scoffs someone in the know.

In September 2015, the website of the magazine *Le Point* published details of the services provided by Denisot: 'Advisory services (contacts with French football authorities and club presidents: PSG, Marseille, etc.), negotiations on the conditions of AS Monaco's participation in French football, remuneration of partners.' Questioned by the weekly magazine, Denisot said: 'Yes, I sent that invoice, which Rybolovlev never paid, but I didn't take offence. I did perform an actual task. At one stage, I wanted to convert to football consultancy, because I know a lot of people. It's the only invoice I have sent in the name of my company SYST MD concerning football. It didn't work out, and I've given up on it.'[57]

Monaco's relations with the league are still not entirely peaceful. But they have stabilised. Once the league understood that Monaco would not move its office to French territory, even if the law ruled against them, a compromise was struck. In January 2014, the league's board of directors, with sixteen votes in favour, four against, and two abstentions, validated

---

[57] On 10 December 2015, Denisot was appointed representative of the French Football Federation on the board of directors of the LFP, the Ligue de Football Professionnel (Professional Football League).

the Monegasque exception, enabling the rules to be modified. In exchange, the club agreed to pay €50 million compensation for its tax and social benefits.

Frédéric Thiriez, president of the league and an individual who maintains very good relations with Prince Albert, was more than a little proud of his actions and of the oral agreement made with his Monegasque counterpart. But the other professional clubs, left out of the negotiations, did not find the conclusion to their taste. Seven clubs (Bordeaux, Lille, Lorient, Caen, Olympique de Marseille, Montpellier, and Paris SG) thought Monaco should pay more. For the boss of Marseille, Vincent Labrune, it made 'no economic sense'.

The seven pursued the case with the Council of State, which was a mistake as, in July 2015, the supreme administrative judge voided the agreement made between the league and Monaco, deeming it 'illicit'. The Council of State held that ASM was under no obligation to have its head office in France.

Farewell, then, to the 'voluntary and definitive' contribution of €50 million Monaco had agreed to pay the forty clubs in Ligues 1 and 2. In another slap in the face for the league, the terms and conditions of convocation of its board of directors modifying the regulation on 23 January 2014 were not deemed satisfactory.

Jean-Michel Aulas, owner and chairman of Olympique Lyonnais, did not enter the anti-Monegasque fray:

My deep-seated belief and strategy has always been to tell

myself that the story with the €50 million constituted two instances of professional misconduct on the part of the league. Firstly, for having chosen the wrong lawyer (who drew up the agreement with Monaco that was denounced by the Council of State) and secondly, for having allowed the seven clubs to attack the league. The latter lost in both form and content, concurring with my initial belief. I stood by Frédéric Thiriez, who is nonetheless a lawyer of the Council of State, which proves that you shouldn't always believe what lawyers say. But Dmitry Rybolovlev and Vadim Vasilyev know that I was the most measured of the club leaders – not to make Monaco happy, but because the whole thing didn't hold water on the legal level.[58]

Vasilyev has turned the page. 'Monaco is an integral part of French football. Everything has settled down. I get on well with most of the club leaders, even those who don't agree, such as Jean-Louis Triaud in Bordeaux. I hope that we have earned their respect.'

Faced with the league's diktat, which followed other signs of defiance, Jean-Marc Goiran feared that Rybolovlev would decide to abandon ship. 'Monaco is a big village where people also like to watch people fall apart. I was afraid that he'd leave when everyone was against him, that his desire and passion had been debilitated, or his enthusiasm cooled.'[59] Rybolovlev, however, has never been easily discouraged.

---

58   Interview with the author.
59   Interview with the author.

CHAPTER 8

PROJECT MONACO: STAGE TWO

Jean-Marc Goiran had another reason to fear that Rybolov-lev might be having second thoughts. The public were not responding to the team's revival. 'Even as we were gunning for PSG, audiences weren't showing up,' he emphasises.

There was no denying Goiran's verdict on the spectators. There were simply not enough of them. One of Monaco's weak links is clearly Stade Louis II. Sited in the neighbourhood of Fontvieille, inaugurated by Prince Rainier in 1985, its perimeter forms a 30,000m² complex, with, in addition to the field ASM trains on, other sports facilities such as the Gaston-Médecin hall and the Prince Albert II water sports centre, a series of office buildings and a parking lot with 1,700 spaces. The latter, however, is under the pitch, which has caused problems with the playing surface. The stadium, located more than eight metres above the roadway level, contains 18,523 seats. That's not many, but as the population is small and the stadium hard to access, even this capacity is rarely utilised. During the 2014–15 season, despite the team finishing third, Stade Louis II was the emptiest stadium in Ligue 1, with an average of 7,825 spectators and a 42.2 per cent occupancy rate.

These logistical problems compound the difficulty of attracting support in a microstate spanning 2 km² with a population of 38,000 – one in three of whom is a millionaire. 'The population base is not huge. That's a problem. Caught between the sea and mountains, Monaco is a unique country,' points out Filips Dhondt, the former CEO of ASM and now advisor to the vice president.

> It's one of our paradoxes: here, people have the financial means but the infrastructures are not compliant with the standards of a club playing in the European Cup. Louis II doesn't have many boxes or luxury lounges. For instance, if Ferrari were to invite sponsors, this would no doubt take place in Monaco. They could imagine a fair where they could store a model, chatting among friends and customers. But we couldn't offer that. It's up to us to work to create new formula and resources, so that we can be self-sufficient.

Wulfran Devauchelle, a consultant in sports economics at international management consulting firm Kurt Salmon, has seen a damper on ASM's growth over the past seven years.

> While the club enjoys an advantageous taxation scheme and an ideal location, it suffers from a lack of transport

infrastructure, a poor window-shopping area, a stadium that is not very modern and whose attendance rate, ticket sales, and premium revenues remain limited. It is complicated to bring in spectators to Louis II, including sponsors. There were, for instances, some talks with Jaguar; they fizzled out. The capacity and dilapidated state of the stadium are handicaps for the 'business seats'. A club such as Manchester United draws 80 per cent of the income from its ticket office from its eight to ten per cent of VIP seats. In Monaco, the ticket revenue revolves around €6 million per year, versus €130 million at Arsenal over the same period.[60]

Rybolovlev is aware of these limitations. He lives in hope of one day investing in the development of the stadium, particularly in VIP boxes. Projects are currently being studied, and discussions are underway, particularly with a London-based architectural firm specialising in sporting arenas. Rybolovlev rarely visits club headquarters in the stadium, where board meetings take place. He prefers to have people visit him at his 2,000m² (including terraces) penthouse.

An effort must also be made regarding the training centre, located since 1981 on the former quarry of La Turbie, a medieval village of 3,000 inhabitants that overlooks the principality. The red-and-whites will never enjoy, as Chelsea does with Cobham, a complex containing thirty playing

---

fields. But Monaco's facilities are reasonably respectable and at least there are no longer prefabs serving as changing rooms, as there were until 2003. That being said, however, despite efforts at refurbishing to comply with standards and extensions, the training centre is still old and pales in comparison to the standards of the top European stars. At Rybolovlev's initiative, several million euros will be invested in renovations.

'The Monaco project is long term,' insists Vasilyev.

> We have been making progress on the training centre, which had become obsolete, even if we train good players at the Academy. We will modernise Stade Louis II. More than the lack of audience, it's the 'quality' of the spectators that we're missing. There is a waiting list for the boxes, but we don't have enough of them. Right now, we only have expensive, uncomfortable, and cramped seating. It's out of the question that we raise the prices for our supporters, but for certain facilities, people are prepared to pay; we can't satisfy their wishes in terms of luxury seating. Football is not just about sport; it's also a social event and a form of entertainment.

Despite these structural handicaps, Monaco's team remains popular.

'ASM is appreciated in France, the proof being its popularity on social networks: the club is the third French club in terms of Facebook fan numbers and the fourth on Twitter,' says Wulfran Devauchelle. 'It is less polarising than PSG, OM or Lyon. Certainly, in terms of "love stakes", Monaco is behind these three but it ties with Saint-Étienne, ahead of Nantes and Bordeaux.'

Media exposure is another way of gaining a reputation and growing income. The club was still in Ligue 2 when Rybolovlev ordered a market study on the possibility that Monaco buys up the international TV rights of its matches. The goal is to develop a platform in certain countries, mainly South America and Asia, allowing matches to be marketed online, on tablets and cell phones. The club was not successful in obtaining its own televisual rights internationally: these are assigned by the league to Qatar-based beIN Sports.[61]

While TV rights were out of Rybolovlev's reach, enhancing the club's global image through the acquisition of star players, and gaining on-field success, was not. Since his takeover, ASM has performed very well. On its return to Ligue 1, armed with new recruits Falcao and James Rodríguez, the club ended the 2013–14 season second behind Paris Saint-Germain. Had Falcao not been injured mid-season, Monaco might even have won the title. Nevertheless, second meant direct qualification for the European Champions

---

61   beIN Sports will pay €80 million per year from 2018 to 2024 for overseas rights. While a substantial increase on the previous €32.5 million it compares unfavourably to the English Premier League, which will earn £1.1 billion a year in overseas rights from 2016 to 2019, with further growth after that already in the pipeline. The Premier League's domestic deal is worth €2 billion a year; Ligue 1's €726 million.

League, providing a financial boon and favourable media exposure.

Somewhat surprisingly, given that Claudio Ranieri had led the club back to the top flight and then achieved their highest points total in Ligue 1 (80), Rybolovlev decided on a change of coach. Before making the decision, the Russian, as usual, took soundings from others with expert insight. Among these was ex-Monaco midfielder Emmanuel Petit. Rybolovlev had been introduced to Petit, Fabien Barthez, and Willy Sagnol, all proud former wearers of the diagonal jersey, at a match at Parc des Princes. Petit was invited to Rybolovlev's duplex.

Scorer of the unforgettable third goal in the 1998 World Cup final against Brazil, the 1,000th goal for Les Bleus, Petit spent twelve years in Monaco. He was trained there, competed in the elite competition from the age of nineteen, made his first start for the national team at twenty, and fleshed out his list of awards (1991 Coupe de France, 1997 Champion de France), before heading to Arsenal, then Barcelona and Chelsea.

The left-footed midfielder with the blond mane spent an hour with Rybolovlev, talking about his change in career and his involvement in the Parisian start-up Netco Sports, the European leader in free mobile and tablet apps devoted to sport. Petit is a shareholder and ambassador for the company, and showed his worth in the latter role by persuading Rybolovlev to add Monaco to the list of clients.[62] 'I don't

---

62   When the app for Monaco was launched in February 2013, Petit kicked off at Stade
      Louis II in the match against Racing Club de Lens.

attend all company meetings, but I insisted on being present for this one; I even paid for my own ticket,' says Petit. 'Like all the Russians I've met, Rybolovlev doesn't talk much, but he is pragmatic and does everything he can to achieve his objectives.'[63]

The two men also talked about football. The Monaco chairman suggested that Petit could take on a role within ASM. 'I didn't ask for anything, though,' says Petit, who outlined his view of the club where he was shaped by Arsène Wenger.

AS Monaco is a microcosm, kind of like AJ Auxerre: a small-town club where it's a complex job to develop the image and marketing, and attract the public as well as sponsors. I described the behind-the-scenes situation to him, explained Monegasque specificities, and made him understand that he had to protect himself, as the French football milieu is quite unusual. He was receptive. He placed Vadim Vasilyev, one of his trusted compatriots, at his side. That was a very clever move. He built up his project in steps. Recruiting Falcao and James Rodríguez was necessary in order to ensure heightened media coverage. Monaco had to be born again from the ashes, like a phoenix. Once he had achieved that, he could move on to the next thing. I do, though, regret that sometimes the club lacks a little humanity. Everything seems closed off to me, few former players stay around, and they

---

63   Interview with the author.

have to be careful not to neglect the training centre. Football has to remain a sport for the people.

Petit told Rybolovlev about his experiences at Chelsea, where his coach for three seasons had been Ranieri.

'I described him as an extraordinary person, with deep humanity. But I also expressed a reservation; he's not able to make his players step up to the next level,' says Petit.

> He can be quite rigid during training, so much so that once, while we were just doing jumps and sprints, I left the session; I wanted to play around, to have fun. He excels at Italian-style physical preparation, but in my opinion, isn't the best person for making a group progress.

The veteran Ranieri was subsequently replaced by 39-year-old Portuguese coach Leonardo Jardim, who was more didactic at heart. Though relatively unknown to most Monaco fans, Jardim was regarded as a coming man by the football cognoscenti. He had impressed with Sporting Braga and Sporting Lisbon in his native country either side of six months at Olympiakós in Greece, where he was sacked despite being ten points clear in the league.

Jardim's early days on the Rock led some to fear the worst: two defeats to open the season and a single victory after five days. 'When we were ranked nineteenth after five days, yes, I could feel the pressure. I can tell you that Rybolovlev was not thrilled … And for me too, personally, it was very hard,' says Vasilyev.

In Jardim's defence, the Monegasque project had abruptly changed shape following the successive departures of Falcao, Abidal, Rodríguez, and Emmanuel Rivière. 'No one had promised him that they'd stay. But he adapted well and made no bones about it,' the vice president adds. 'We had to take the risk of a profound and rapid upheaval.'

'It was very important to find the right coach,' Vasilyev told the *Daily Telegraph* later.

When we set out to bring in Leonardo Jardim we discussed many times the philosophy so that he understood it and it has really been a huge pleasure to work with him. He will never say 'why are you selling this player?' He understands it's part of this project. Our revenues were not growing the way we projected – sponsors were not queuing up, the stadium, it's quite old, too small. So we had to change the project. It was dramatic, drastic, yes, but now we have the right model – sporting and financial – for our type of club.

This model says that we have to develop young players because if we want to play at the highest level we should compensate for the revenues that we don't have from sponsorship or match days with money through the transfer market. If not, we would have to scale down. It means we have to work well in planning and developing – and at a certain point letting them go.

Monaco's problem was the new regulation of Financial Fair Play instituted by UEFA, European football's governing body. This controversial policy dictated that a club should not spend more than it earned, with threats of punishment including exclusion. This was a hammer blow for a club such as Monaco, with its limited revenue streams, and was also unpopular at other clubs backed by super-rich benefactors, such as Manchester City. UEFA's argument was that it prevented clubs from overreaching themselves and going into debt – European football had a huge collective debt. However, to others it seemed aimed at preserving the status quo and preventing others from gatecrashing the elite.

The FFP obliged Monaco to rein in their spending, now favouring hopefuls over confirmed stars. This modification of the business model became indispensable, since UEFA didn't trifle when it came to regulations. In May 2014, Manchester City and Paris Saint-Germain were among nine clubs punished. Both were fined €60 million and suffered further spending curbs and squad limitations.

A year later Monaco were among ten clubs sanctioned, including Inter Milan, Roma, Besiktas, and Lokomotiv Moscow. Monaco were fined €13 million and told to reduce their squad for European competition from the customary twenty-five players to twenty-two. Monaco also agreed to limit their deficit to €15 million for the next two financial years, breaking even in time for the 2017–18 season. The club's communiqué stated: 'Following considerable efforts made this season, heavier sanctions were avoided. This decision reaffirms the club's decision to reshape its project. AS Monaco has always affirmed its desire to comply with the criteria imposed by the FFP and will continue to maintain this strategy in the future.'

There were already signs that the team would remain competitive despite the change in policy. On the domestic front in 2014–15 Monaco finished third in Ligue 1, behind PSG and Lyon, thus qualifying for a Champions League play-off. In that competition they reached the semi-finals, knocking out Arsenal with a dramatic 3–1 win at the Emirates en route. Juventus, as they would again in the following season, proved too wily, but a 1–0 aggregate defeat was an honourable exit, sweetened by competition earnings of around €45 million.

That was enough to encourage Monaco to extend Leonardo Jardim's contract until 2019, and to step up their shift in approach. It was farewell to the veteran Dimitar Berbatov, young talents Anthony Martial and Geoffrey Kondogbia, plus the likes of Aymen Abdennour and Lucas Ocampos. The replacements were, in general, less heralded. The main exceptions were Fábio Coentrão, who had won trophies with Real Madrid, and Stephan El Shaarawy, who had forged a reputation in Italy. Both players, however, were not in as much demand as previously.

In total Monaco spent €70 million but raised €200 million: a European record. *France Football* analysed player movements since Rybolovlev had become chairman: 197

transactions, including transfers, loans, loan returns, and acquisitions of free players. Spending was estimated to be €334 million and sales at €276 million. When, on 28 August 2015, nineteen-year-old Portuguese midfielder Rony Lopes signed for five years from Manchester City, Jardim summed up ASM's modus operandi, where players are trained to maturity to better sell them, and where speculation counts at least as much as sporting ability.

'This is all part of the club's business,' Jardim said. 'Rony has to recognise the work and the methodology that there is in Monaco. To do that, it'll take five or six months. Then we'll see in January if we'll consider a loan.'

Jardim is lucid; he has come to realise that anything can happen within his team and that, for economic reasons, it is not unlikely that five or six players under contract, the team's star players, might suddenly disappear. This is part and parcel of Monaco's project, closely supervised by UEFA within the FFP rules and a policy forced by the limitations of ticket sales and sponsorship.

That's why the club wants to keep mistakes to a minimum in its recruitment of young hopefuls. Key to this process has been Luis Campos. Now an advisor to Lille, Campos was sports advisor, then technical director at Monaco from 2013–2016. He was hired by Vasilyev after working in his native Portugal, then under Mourinho at Real Madrid. Initially Campos worked with Claudio Ranieri and his predecessor as technical director, Riccardo Pecini. When these men both

left, in the summer of 2014, Campos took over as technical
director charged with executing the new transfer policy.

In an interview with Yahoo! Sport in May 2017, Campos
said:

> From one moment to the other the ability to invest in con-
> firmed talents disappeared and I saw many people despair.
> If we wanted to continue at the highest level, we had to rad-
> ically change policy and find young talents, put them in a
> good showcase, and then sell to make strong financial con-
> tributions to sustain the project. I stopped living day to day
> at the club, and began living in airplanes, hotels and stadiums
> all around the world – which harmed me later. Fortunately,
> Vadim relied on me and my choices. Only twice did he hes-
> itate because he listened to others and lost the business of
> two current superstars, but that served as an example for the
> immense trust he then deposited in me. Vadim contributed a
> lot with his tremendous negotiating skills and diplomacy, but
> our ability to recruit well at low prices was decisive.

Under Campos six scouts were charged with scouring the
world's football fields to look for new pearls, while also
supervising the many players out on loan. Organised in a
near-scientific manner, Campos had a list of nine potential
successors for each position in the team. Players were cate-
gorised according to their likely purchase prices. Three out
of each nine had a value of below €6 million, three values of

€6 million to €10 million, and three values above that. According to Monegasque needs and finances, Vasilyev, with Rybolovlev's consent, only had to 'pluck' a player from the list to negotiate a transfer or loan.

The club has become a master in the art of investing in order to better resell, including players whose purchase price may have seemed high at the time. Examples include Tunisian defender Abdennour, who signed with Monaco in 2014 from Toulouse for €15 million and was transferred to Valencia for double that in August 2015: an agreement worked out over lunch with Valencia's owner, Singaporean billionaire Peter Lim, during the Champions League play-off between the two teams. The midfielder Kondogbia, who came from Seville in the summer of 2013 for €20 million, was sold for twice as much to Inter Milan two years later.

'Working with Luis Campos is a pleasure. He's such a hard worker and a courteous professional who knows the market and the players,' says agent Christophe Hutteau, who notably advised Mathieu Valbuena for eight years.

I suggested a Russian hopeful to him who was on my books, Andrei Panyukov, a forward playing in Lithuania. He answered by email: 'My dear Christophe, I know this kid. We've been watching him for six months.'[64] And Monaco was the

---

64   Panyukov was eventually loaned to fellow Ligue 1 club AC Ajaccio, then Sporting Braga, in Portugal, but failed to make an impact at either and returned to Lithuania.

only French club to send an emissary to the Under-20 World Cup in New Zealand in June 2015. Their project is coherent and pertinent. Even when they refuse a player from me, they always do so with style.[65]

Campos himself told Yahoo! Sport:

Not everyone can be a good football player, nor a good doctor or engineer. So not everyone can have this ability to identify good players who are able to join and form a good team. [It] is a complex process that comes not just from the choice of good players, but also from our ability to predict who will interact well with whom. It's like forming a jigsaw puzzle: the right pieces, in the right places.

Until the flowering of the extraordinary team of 2016–17, Monaco were unable to stop the domestic domination of PSG, who won four consecutive titles (2012–16). But Paris had a €500 million budget, compared to €130 million for Monaco in 2015–16.

'We are not jealous of PSG,' affirms Vasilyev. 'Our initial project may've resembled theirs, but we don't share the same vision. Our economic models are totally different. Recruiting Falcao or Rodríguez was important but not viable over the long term, with the lack of revenue and sponsors, plus

---

65   Interview with the author.

Financial Fair Play. We could not retain our major players. Paris is the club of the capital; its shareholder is a very wealthy state. We are ambitious but also realistic.'

Prior to usurping PSG in Ligue 1 in 2017, Monaco found other ways to promote themselves. They posed for the official team photo at the Opera of Monte Carlo; the team's jersey with its name in velvet was given to Pharrell Williams, the man behind the smash hit 'Happy', at his concert; and portraits of the club's stars, such as Michel Hidalgo, Manuel Amoros, and Glenn Hoddle, were displayed in the corridors of the Stade Louis II.

Also included in this historic fresco is Jean Petit. Aged sixty-six, Petit still lives on the Rock. Born in Toulouse, a midfielder with France at the 1978 World Cup, he moved to Monaco as a young pro and never left. Petit spent his whole career on the Rock playing 428 matches: a proud captain, and winner of two championship titles and one Coupe de France. ASM's 'Swiss army knife', Jean Petit then joined the staff to recruit young hopefuls, a then inchoate profession. Deputy coach to Arsène Wenger, Jean Tigana, Didier Deschamps, Ricardo, Marco Simone, and Claudio Ranieri, he was even caretaker coach twice, in 1994 and 2005. His job now involves coaching the players who aren't chosen for the first team and monitoring those out on loan.

Petit has seen club leaders come and go. With the arrival of Rybolovlev in December 2011, he was initially wary. Petit was nearing the end of his contract and feared there would be a purge.

'His arrival was presented to us as a Christmas present, given that the club was in such bad shape financially and on a sporting level. We immediately wondered how long he'd stay and if the old staff would still be welcome, even if history can't just be wiped out in one go,' Petit recalls.

> During the first match, in Istres, he greeted us in the changing room and said a few words. He also came to training sessions. But he tends to delegate. Campora visited once a week at La Turbie. He wanted to know everything and he knew everyone; right down to the storekeeper.[66]

Petit started to view Rybolovlev differently after he took such a strong stand in opposing the transfer of ASM's head office to France.

> He earned everyone's respect in his fight against the league and by refusing the €200 million Le Graët demanded. Monegasques enjoy fighting solo against the rest of the world. Charles Campora, Jean-Louis's father, who was also a chairman in the fifties, had already threatened to play in the Italian championship. We'd been hearing for ages that the

---

66   Interview with the author.

club had had preferential treatment thanks to the special status of the principality.

This constancy in battle unites the Monegasques, as does the sustained connection between the club and the Palace. Petit, who arrived at ASM as a player in 1969, had already been invited to the Palace by Prince Rainier so that the latter could probe his thoughts after the draw for a competition.

'I was the captain and he told his secretary "Bring Jean up to see me,"' says Petit.

He invited the team over after a Coupe de France match, promising us a feast of spit-roasted mutton each time we got through to the next round. We reached the final of the competition and we played petanque while Princess Grace was preparing the meal. Things were different back then.

He also bumped into Prince Rainier one late afternoon on Larvotto Beach. Petit was sitting at the bar, waiting for an appointment. 'When he saw me, he asked: "What's wrong with the team?" I was uncomfortable.'

Petit was consumed by the same sense of urgency and focus when he met Dmitry Rybolovlev. 'As with Prince Rainier, when you see him, you know that you'll have five minutes to describe the situation. You mustn't make false statements or get carried away, or bad-mouth anyone,' he explains.

The man who had known Prince Albert as a child did

not hesitate to call on the assistance of the Prince soon after Rybolovlev's arrival. During half time at a Ligue 2 match (which he attended with former player Delio Onnis, an Italian-Argentinian who scored a record 299 goals in the French championship), Petit crossed paths with the Prince.

'I asked him to introduce Delio and myself. We didn't want to disturb him but wanted him to understand what we were doing. I told the Prince that, possibly, Rybolovlev didn't know who we were. "You're kidding me," he replied. And he introduced us in the lounge.'

Prince Albert, even if he no longer sits on the board of directors, is never far away when it comes to ASM. When he was younger, he would sometimes even pass the ball around a bit with players during training. Today, he keeps an eye on the club, but from a greater distance. He no longer pulls strings behind the scenes, although he is still consulted and retains certain prerogatives. He was the one who ensured that Frédéric Barilaro, the board member who had been dismissed in May 2012 along with Marco Simone (for whom he was the deputy), was reinstated at ASM. Prince Albert's intervention enabled Barilaro to recover his role as the director of the training centre. He has since been replaced by Nicolas Weber and now holds the position of technical director at the Academy, while also supervising the U19 nationals.

After the surprise success at Arsenal in the Champions League in February 2015 the Prince went across the pitch over to thank the 3,000 Monegasque supporters who'd made the trip to the Emirates Stadium. The delighted royal also kissed the cheeks of two former members of the club, Ludovic Giuly and Sonny Anderson, who were consultants that evening for beIN Sports, then had his photograph taken in the Monaco dugout.

The ties between Albert II and Rybolovlev are regularly reported as having been loosened, and that the honeymoon phase is over. On several occasions, the Prince has commented on the matter. In the *Journal du Dimanche* in March 2015, he was questioned about his role at the club and said that he is still consulted.

Perhaps less frequently than in the past, but we do still hold regular meetings with Mr Rybolovlev and Mr Vasilyev about overall strategy as well as about the choices of players and the coach. I have heard it said that I'd learned about the arrival of Jardim through the press. That is false. I was told beforehand. ... Parting with James Rodríguez or lending Falcao are choices relating to opportunities that probably shouldn't be missed. Unlike what I may have read; there has never been any question of Rybolovlev abandoning the club and leaving the principality.

Regarding these same areas of tension, Prince Albert had already spoken out in November 2014 on the Canal+ television channel. 'There have never been hidden areas between us. ... Naturally, I am kept informed of any major developments and key decisions to be made. Things are done cooperatively; we exchange ideas and the decisions are mostly made together.'

Prince Albert made another statement on 1 July 2015, in a lounge at the Monaco Yacht Club, at the invitation of the principality's Press Club. Several days prior to the festivities organised for the tenth anniversary of his reign, he once again spelled out his thoughts on the subject: 'These stories about not getting along with Mr Rybolovlev are pure inventions on the part of your colleagues. I have regularly been kept informed regarding decisions made by the leaders and the various strategies of ASM.'

These recurrent rumours have their corollary: in taking control of AS Monaco, Rybolovlev was apparently dreaming of obtaining a Monegasque passport, which would enable him to enjoy more lenient tax conditions. For *Le Monde*, this 'invaluable foot-in-the-door would enable him to shelter his Cypriot assets'. Only Prince Albert has the ability to deliver passports and does so sparingly. He broached the issue on Canal +: 'There is a very specific set of criteria for a request for naturalisation and the whole process that goes along with that. In fact, that's an issue that has never been on the table.' The TV journalist repeated the question, asking if this eventuality had not yet cropped up because Rybolovlev had not lived on the Rock for ten years.

'Among other things, yes,' Prince Albert responded.

Rybolovlev says: 'My relationship with Prince Albert is a good and cordial one. It is true that I was looking to obtain the Monegasque passport but that is absolutely unrelated to the fact of having taken over the club. It was not included in the transaction.'[67]

Is it simply a matter of prestige? At any rate, Rybolovlev has held a Cypriot passport since 2010, which makes him a citizen of the European Union. Most of his fortune is placed in trusts on the island, where he funded the renovation of the Orthodox Cathedral of Limassol and acquired 9.7 per cent of the Bank of Cyprus for €223 million.

---

67   Interview with the author.

CHAPTER 9

IMAGE CONTROL

Some football club owners like the limelight that the world's most popular game provides. Alan Sugar received a degree of attention as founder and owner of electronics company Amstrad, but he only escaped the business pages when he became owner of Tottenham Hotspur. He did not like much of the resultant publicity – it was a controversial period for the club – but some doubt he would have become a reality TV star without the football connection. Michael Knighton's brief period at Manchester United was notable for publicity-seeking escapades, while Olympique Lyonnais' Jean-Michel Aulas is a social media enthusiast.

Most owners, however, prefer the shadows. 'Silent Stan' Kroenke has said little since becoming Arsenal's major shareholder, the Manchester United-owning Glazer family are similarly reticent, and Roman Abramovich has not given an interview in a dozen years at Chelsea. Dmitry Rybolovlev is slightly more talkative, but not much. Since he became chairman of AS Monaco in December 2011 he has given barely a handful of interviews: one each with *Paris Match*, *L'Équipe*, *Nice-Matin* (he was practically obliged, given the regional proximity), and *Monaco-Matin*. The latter was a double-page spread in which he talked about his support for some of the projects of Les Ballets de Monte-Carlo, whose director, choreographer Jean-Christophe Maillot,[68] he appreciates greatly; some of the charitable organisations he backs, including the Monaco Red Cross and Fight Aids Monaco; and the installation on the Rock of the Monaco Mission Centre for Solar Impulse 2, a project set up in conjunction with the Prince Albert II of Monaco Foundation to send a solar-powered plane around the globe.

Referring to his reluctance to engage in society life, he summarised his feelings: 'I have an active life, but my priorities are business and family. That determines all the rest.'

Later in 2015, he also commented on the Bouvier affair – where he bought artworks through a Swiss art dealer he now suspects of fraud. It was the first opportunity to put his view on the case to a television camera, as part of TF1's news programme, *Sept à huit*. The seventeen-minute programme aired on 20 December, entitled 'A $500 million scam?'

Keeping an eye on the media for Rybolovlev is Sergey Chernitsyn. A Moscow native and political science expert

---

68 In June 2015, Rybolovlev's lawyer, Tetiana Bersheda, was elected as head of the association of Friends of the Ballets de Monte-Carlo. Two months later Bersheda, a passionate ballet fan, revealed Rybolovlev would be funding a tour to Cuba by the Ballets of Monte-Carlo and an exceptional evening for the dancers with the famous Buena Vista Social Club.

with a degree in eastern studies and philology, he is also a poacher turned gamekeeper having once been an economic journalist. Juggling between languages and time zones, he keeps an eye on anything to do with 'DR', or 'the chairman', as he also calls Rybolovlev.

'It's true, the chairman doesn't like to communicate,' said Chernitsyn.

> For example, he never talks to the Russian media. When he commented on the listing of part of Uralkali's capital on the London exchange, it was because he had to: those are the rules when listing on the London Stock Exchange. He doesn't appreciate when his private life is intruded upon – he expects it to be respected. On the other hand, while it's indeed rare that he speaks to the press, when he does, he's entirely frank.[69]

Chernitsyn added, 'While he doesn't speak in public, he has the rare talent of knowing how to listen. And even though he is involved in projects across the globe, he still has a profoundly Russian soul … He is very proud of his roots and would never betray them.'

AS Monaco's image is orchestrated by Bruno Skropeta, head of communications and marketing for the brand (at this level, a club is considered a brand). Another ex-journalist,

---

69   Interview with the author.

he swapped sides after Euro 2008, initially joining Paris Saint-Germain as head of communications and (also involvement with marketing).

During the next four years he dealt with the change of ownership from American (Colony Capital was the major shareholder) to Qatari hands (QSI, the sovereign wealth fund) and the coming and going of a string of managers (Paul Le Guen, Antoine Kombouaré, and Carlo Ancelotti). In July 2012, the Monaco directors convinced him to join their project, even though the club hadn't yet returned to elite level. He thus went from a group owned by a state to another belonging, via a trust, to a businessman. The two clubs each have immensely wealthy owners, both of whom are casually investing to build up their teams. But those are not the only things they have in common, says Skropeta.

Both Dmitry Rybolovlev and the Qataris think big. In terms of their mentality, they don't dwell on the details. A typical French reaction in regard to certain initiatives on the transfer market would be to say, 'No, that's impossible; it'll never work', but not them. They have the same goal – to give themselves the means to carry out their ambitions, while remaining coherent and pragmatic. In Monaco, they have mapped out an ideal trajectory that corresponds to the scenario the chairman imagined to return the club to its proud origins: move up to Ligue 1, sign up big players, compete in the Champions League, and be a key player on the European scene. Certainly there have been a few changes, but the club is building itself up steadily.[70]

Bruno Skropeta leads a department that has grown from two to twelve people since his arrival three and a half years ago. ASM's website is now translated into five languages, including Russian; they have 1.5 million followers on Twitter (up from only 1,000 in 2012), 4.6 million on Facebook, and 524,000 on Instagram. They have channels on YouTube and Sound-Cloud, and a presence on Snapchat and LinkedIn. There is a daily series where the players (frontline ambassadors) are asked to participate in various ways, such as in online chats where they reply to fans, who also have an opportunity to win shirts.

That is the price that must be paid for Monegasque-style storytelling to succeed. A 360-degree model that recounts the club's saga in different ways, creating emotion that fans can identify with and, if possible, monetising that passion and generating revenue. Among the initiatives designed to extend the reach of the club's brand are a digital agreement with noted Brazilian club Cruzeiro, of Belo Horizonte, and participation in the Copa EuroAmerica, a friendly football exhibition tournament that took place in Colombia in 2014.

Although not involved on a daily basis, Rybolovlev is in firm control, obsessed with every detail and wanting to be

---

70   Interview with the author.

made aware of everything that matters. The club has really got under his skin. Even in Ligue 2 he wanted to follow every game live, whether on his yacht in the Caribbean, in his chalet in Gstaad, on the island of Skorpios, or at his dacha in Moscow. Eurosport, broadcaster of the Monday night matches, finally gave him a tablet with a private code. Prior to being revamped, the club's website had bugs, and when he was not able to connect from any point on the globe, particularly when the league tables were published, he became annoyed.

Although in the principality the latest fashion is to stick the badge of the Automobile Club (organiser of the Formula 1 Grand Prix and Monte-Carlo Rally) on the back of your car, Rybolovlev ordered badges with the ASM logo for himself and his close friends. A few months later, the club changed its graphic design, and Rybolovlev had to order new ones. Not that this caught him by surprise – he was present at the tender meeting for the logo change. When a model was presented using 3D, he rejected it, commenting that 3D would soon be outdated.

Skropeta says Rybolovlev brings a positive pressure to the club, which will help it to move forward.

He takes things seriously and, during meetings, soon identifies where the problems lie. His support is ongoing. He assimilates things quickly, and once they have been fully discussed, he brings all his means to bear. He listens carefully, asks lots of questions, and then makes a firm decision. He's a fighting machine. He's not just a shareholder who determines the strategy. If he seems detached from the outside, that's not the case. The third of every month, we send him analysis and summaries of our social networks. If by the fourth he hasn't received anything, he asks why it wasn't done the day before.

So, Rybolovlev is certainly involved, but he is scarcely visible in the media. Instead, he lets Vadim Vasilyev be the figurehead of the board. It is Vasilyev who poses for photographs with the new recruits at their official presentations, even on the occasion of the transfer that stunned Europe, the acquisition of Falcao. But the latter was as much a gesture by Rybolovlev to his friend as a desire to stay in the shadows. Vasilyev, spontaneous, forthcoming, and formidably intelligent, understands.

In the beginning, I was continually asked why the chairman didn't comment. It became very tiresome. Those questions are rarer today. Everyone has their own personality. It's not the chairman's role, and it's just not his thing. Dmitry is passionate about the club, so it's up to everyone to respect his way of doing things. Dealing with the press has nothing to do with passion. It causes lots of rumours and results in all sorts of articles. That doesn't worry me, though. It's the media's job to find subjects and stories. With all the transfers, the first year was pretty mad, but now things have calmed down. It's not worth reacting to each announcement. The important thing is to have a serious and intelligent plan, which demonstrates our savoir-faire.[71]

Obviously it's not easy to be head of communications of a club whose chairman avoids the microphone. Skropeta remembers his first meeting at the Monaco apartment of Rybolovlev, who knew everything about him ('Not only my CV, but also what other people said about me') and was looking for someone 'who wasn't afraid of voicing their opinion.'

Initially I favoured the approach that the chairman should speak, but now I have accepted that he doesn't. He understands that can cause frustration [for the media] but that's the way he is.

Rybolovlev doesn't want to engage with the media. It's not a superiority complex; it's just his way of doing things. He gets the articles about the club translated and asks us about them. He doesn't complain about the often harsh way in which he's treated, but tries to understand why the journalists claim this or that; why, and in which context. It's a sign of intelligence. Given that he doesn't want to share his feelings, he has to understand that 80 per cent of what's written about him will contain mistakes. The most important thing is that it doesn't put him off. With such a personality, we have to face up to a lot of rumours, theories, and suspicions. There's

---

71 Interview with the author.

an element of fantasy, associated with a lack of understanding or ignorance. But although we can't dictate everything that's written about the club, we can at least control the message and choose the moment it's delivered.

The official AS Monaco TV channel has also had to become more upmarket. The directing, production, and post-production of content are mostly carried out by Monaco Broadcast. Stéphane Morandi is the CEO and managing director. Everyone on the Rock claims to be close to Prince Albert, but Morandi is a real friend, so much so that the Prince was present in January 2013 for the inauguration of the company's 280-square metre television studio. Until then, ASM had a poor website, Morandi explains.

Dmitry Rybolovlev wanted to create web TV and his wishes were granted three years ago. He's both passionate about ASM and a businessman. Working with him is easy because he loves football. Monaco is his club; he has invested a lot into it. He has a warm and respectful relationship with the Palace, which is indispensable. Rybolovlev doesn't often go out to restaurants, and even less to nightclubs, but he is appreciated in the principality, where everyone knows one another. The club is well organised, and I am mostly in touch with Vadim Vasilyev.[72]

---

72   Interview with the author.

But even with the club's television channel, Rybolovlev keeps his usual distance.

> He certainly doesn't like to show off. The only time he spoke in public was to announce the arrival of Falcao, under the circus tent at Fontvieille. But, after having followed a match between Bastia and Monaco on a telephone screen in a Madrid restaurant, where we were attending a summit between Real and Barcelona, I saw at first hand how passionate he was about it. Just like the Prince, in fact. They are reserved in public, but are more expansive in private and in the stadium.

Rybolovlev has now accepted, whether he likes it or not, that being chairman of a club like Monaco makes him a public personality. But he still cultivates a mysterious side and fully intends to control his communications. He doesn't deem it worthwhile or strategic to get involved with media hype, especially as he only speaks Russian – even if his close entourage is composed of polyglots Vasilyev, Bersheda, and Chernitsyn. The language barrier inevitably hinders dialogue with non-Russian speakers. Lately Rybolovlev has started working hard at English classes again. He does speak English, which he uses in private, but as long as he doesn't speak it perfectly, he refuses to use it, at least in public.

'The problem is it's difficult for all these foreign words to find a path in my head. I think a lot, my thoughts jostle against one another in my brain – so much so that there's no room for English,'[73] he says.

It's unclear whether he's joking or not.

Aulas has his own ideas on the subject. 'When we talk, he always has an interpreter, but I can assure you he understands English. We had lunch in early summer at La Marée, an excellent fish, seafood, and caviar restaurant at the port of Monaco. Through our wine and meal choices, I was able to confirm that he understood English, and even a few words in French.'[74]

If talking to the press is a burden, imagine Rybolovlev's absolute horror at being photographed. He avoids camera lenses and asking him to pose for a picture is usually pointless. Franck Nataf nevertheless managed, during a private meeting at his home, to get a smile out of his then boss: Nataf was the club's official photographer for almost two seasons. Formerly at the *Parisien* and *L'Équipe*, Nataf is clearly used to uncompromising personalities – he officiated at Nicolas Anelka's wedding!

Seasoned photographer Bernard Sidler, who has covered the Gulf War and conflicts in Rwanda, the Sahel, and the former Yugoslavia, and who more recently was the sole photographer to accompany French Special Forces in Iraq, has been the most successful at establishing an intimate relationship with the AS Monaco chairman. The result: six pages

---

73   Interview with the author.
74   Interview with the author.

in *Paris Match* in November 2013. Among the images were Rybolovlev in his 1,600m² lounge-study in front of three television screens (all showing different programmes); on the balcony of his penthouse with a view over the harbour and the Palace; in his tracksuit in his apartment's fitness room with his daughter Ekaterina; and with striker Falcao at the Hotel Métropole before dining at Robuchon. But to achieve all this required a year of negotiation by Sidler and the journalist who conducted the interview, Ghislaine Ribeyre (who sadly died, aged just forty-one, seventeen months later after a long battle with illness).

'Dmitry Rybolovlev has little experience with the media, and like most Russians, he likes to take his time,' Sidler recalls.

Thanks to the tact and elegance of Ghislaine, whom we miss, we were able to make contact and meet his entourage, as I had also been recommended by the Palace (Sidler exhibited at the Atrium of the Monte-Carlo casino). It was important to establish a relationship built on trust; it's the key to everything. For *Match*, photographs are essential. Then, one day, we got the green light.[75]

The weekly magazine got the exclusive scoop, ousting its competitor *Vanity Fair*. Sidler arrived in the principality with his assistant and stayed for four days. At the first meeting, he

---

75 Interview with the author.

outlined his vision, in particular the importance of making it a pleasure for Rybolovlev. 'He understood that we were professionals,' says the photographer.

> I knew that it would make him stressed, so I tried to relax him by reassurng him, guiding him, explaining to him how to relax his face and then we tried it together. Rybolovlev portrays the image of being a man of ice, and, like many of his compatriots, he isn't very expressive. But, once he agreed to play along, he did so wholeheartedly. He was intelligent enough to let us lead the way and had complete faith in us. Like Tony Blair and the King of Morocco Mohammed VI, both of whom I have photographed, he was relaxed and patient; and he behaved like a gentleman. He allowed us to enter his private world, and during the meals we shared, was charming, talking about his life and the difficulties he has faced, including his time in prison.

Falcao, when he was contacted and asked to pose beside the chairman and his daughter, needed no encouragement, doing so with a broad smile. Satisfied with the article, Rybolovlev's team warmly thanked the *Paris Match* duo.

'This assignment was such a pleasure. He's not a show-off, not at all nouveau riche. He prefers being discreet and relies on a remarkable team that organises things around him. The three days of meetings took place without a hiccup, and I was even able to make him laugh,' says Sidler.

Rybolovlev's relationship with journalists is consistent in its non-existence. But, occasionally some get further than just a simple handshake – for example, Charles Villeneuve, former head of sports at TF1, the television channel for which he presented various programmes. Villeneuve was also briefly president of Paris Saint-Germain. Between the aloof Russian and the extrovert, loquacious Oriental – born in Lebanon to an Armenian mother – there was an immediate connection. Villeneuve, with his ability for decoding situations and knowing how to handle people, even visited Rybolovlev's yacht moored off the private island of Skorpios, the day after Ekaterina's twenty-fifth birthday. Their exchanges don't deal with communications or the media, but with politics, Villeneuve explains.

Yes, politics in its broadest sense, including geopolitics, from the Near East to Russia. Our discussions range from Putin's personality to the sale of Mistral helicopter carriers. We saw each other three or four times when he arrived in Monaco, and he questioned me about how our country works. I told him that football is a kind of indirect form of diplomacy and that the problem with France is that politicians love to get involved, for example, the public-private partnerships for the construction of stadiums, even though owning your own stadium is vital.

Initially, given the threat of financial fair play and the fact that everyone was trying to pick a quarrel with him, I didn't understand what Rybolovlev hoped to gain from the club. We talked about other clubs opposing ASM and the fact that, after tax, a French team spends four times more than any English club. I got to know him; he is clever and thinks quickly, his capacity for reaction is astonishing. He's nice, not at all bling-bling. He asked me direct questions; I gave straight answers.[76]

Even though Villeneuve was president of PSG for eight and a half months between 2008 and 2009, and was present for PSG's signing of Ludovic Giuly and Claude Makelele, Rybolovlev never asked him 'questions about Paris Saint-Germain', the commentator says.

But on the other hand, he was curious to know more about how the men directing football were organised and their political implications. It was the opportunity to inform him that Noël Le Graët, the Federation president, was a socialist mayor of Guingamp (from 1995 to 2008) and had supported François Hollande since the primary elections. Football and politics are closely related. It's up to him whether he takes an interest in things rather than turning away. He never recounted his previous life in Russia to me; our discussions were confined to current affairs. He consulted me in my capacity as a journalist, nothing more. I didn't organise any meetings for him.

---

76   Interview with the author.

Not even meetings with Villeneuve's friend Arsène Wenger, manager of Arsenal (and formerly of Monaco), 'an extraordinary trainer and man,' who hosts Villeneuve at his home in London, and who stays with Villeneuve when in Paris.

But Villenueve did help to cancel Monaco's February 2015 loan of Dominique Pando to national league club Paris FC, which would have prevented ASM from lending Lucas Ocampos to Marseille. The league would not have ratified the latter deal as regulations stipulate that a team can only 'temporarily transfer seven of its licensed players' and ASM had already used up its quota.

Rybolovlev's reluctance to engage with the media also meant it took time to win the trust and support of the club's fans; because, yes, they do exist, and they are the subject of repeated jokes. Not so long ago, on the French radio station RTL, Bernard Tapie, who when he was president of Marseille battled it out with Monaco for the title, said: 'At OM, fans know the name and age of players. At Monaco, it's the opposite!'

It's a hackneyed joke that guarantees laughs, but it does depict a certain reality. During the 2014–15 season in Ligue 1, Monaco attracted an average crowd of 7,825 to a stadium that can hold 18,523 spectators. Even in the championship year of 2016–17 Louis II had the lowest attendances of any Ligue 1 club, an average of 9,499, below even the relegated teams, making them the least supported French champions ever. This means a large number of yellow seats are left vacant, and inevitably, the atmosphere at the stadium is affected.

Rybolovlev does take steps to entice fans. When he took over the club, he immediately demanded that management meet with supporters' clubs and identify their needs. And, even though he doesn't like communicating, he insisted that the information make its way up, so that the motivation of 'ultras' could be understood, along with how best to improve the situation. He also refused to remove (as a sponsor had wished) the diagonal design on the jersey, with red at the top and white below – a registered design that is part of ASM's history, created by Princess Grace in 1960. He was present at the inauguration of a club boutique in town. The fact that Rybolovlev avoids the media doesn't worry Jean-Paul Chaude, head of the Monaco Supporters' Club.

'We can't stop people from talking, but it's the results that count,' he told *Le Monde*. In 1986, his 'ultra' group in Monaco was the first to be created, along with the Sconvolts in Cagliari.

For example, no one knows the president of Arsenal. We don't care about him, or about management. What matters is the continuity of the project. People come and go, but what is most important is the entity, the ASM brand. It's better to work in the shadows, concentrate on the objectives, and not show off in the press.

Message received, loud and clear.

CHAPTER 10

PRESIDENTIAL FRIENDS AND RIVALS

With one of his four mobile phones permanently affixed to his ear, Jorge Mendes, a 51-year-old Portuguese playboy with a weathered face, is the most influential sports agent in the world. A former third-division goalkeeper, then video store and nightclub manager, he now runs multinational Gestifute, whose annual turnover for 2014 totalled €536 million.[77] His player portfolio is far-reaching, with commission fees to match. Among his clients are Argentinian winger Ángel Di María, who transferred from Manchester United to Paris Saint-Germain for €63 million in August 2015, Brazilian-born Spanish striker Diego Costa, and Chelsea manager José Mourinho. But the real cream of the crop in his list of big-name clients is his compatriot Cristiano Ronaldo, the star of Real Madrid, triple winner of the Ballon d'Or, and godfather to Mendes's son.

---

77   According to *Forbes*, Mendes pocketed US$95.6 million (€84 million) in commission via Gestifute in 2015. However, he is not the highest-earning agent in the world. American Scott Boras, an ex-lawyer specialising in the pharmaceutical sector who represents several top-flight baseball players, still outearns Mendes.

Undeniably blessed with the gift of the gab, in February 2015, during an interview for ESPN, Mendes named the club presidents who, in his opinion, deserved special credit:

> We are in the midst of a major financial crisis and these people have saved football. We must therefore offer [our] heartfelt thanks to Roman Abramovich at Chelsea; Sheikh Mansour at Manchester City; Nasser al-Khelaïfi at PSG; Dmitry Rybolovlev at Monaco; and Peter Lim at Valencia. Do you know what their clubs were like before they came? All you need to do is ask their supporters whether they would like to go back to the way it was before.

Supporters of those clubs may well agree, although other football fans and observers clearly do not welcome wealthy foreign owners uncritically. But Mendes is not exactly objective in his views. An investment fund advisor who also engages in Third Party Ownership (TPO) (even though it was banned by FIFA and described by Michel Platini as 'a kind of slavery'),[78] Mendes negotiated with all the names he quoted and one would imagine profited handsomely from the association. That is not to suggest the clubs have not benefited from his presence, too. Mendes has a large network of influential contacts and assists in recruiting players that clubs might otherwise struggle to sign.

---

78 Third-party ownership occurs when the true 'owner' of a player is not only the club, but also companies or private investors that hold a share of the rights.

Mendes has certainly been a key figure in AS Monaco's often impressive new signings. During the team's rise through Ligue 1, he sold the team three players for €130 million: Radamel Falcao (€60 million), João Moutinho (€45 million), and James Rodríguez (€25 million). In the same summer of 2013, more of his clients moved to Monaco, including experienced player Ricardo Carvalho as a free transfer and the up-and-coming Fabinho. Since then, Nigerian Elderson Echiejile, Brazilian Wallace, and Portuguese Bernardo Silva (an excellent find, who would realise an enormous profit when sold in 2017), previously unknown Monegasque recruits, now bear the Mendes label, too.

Among ASM's 2015 summer recruits were two Portuguese 21-year-olds whose careers benefited from their time at the club. Hélder Costa was on loan from Benfica, while Ivan Cavaleiro was purchased from the Portugese powerhouse for a fee of €15 million. And let's not forget the arrival, on loan, of Real Madrid's Fábio Coentrão.

Mendes's relationship with ASM goes way back. The super agent's career really took off in 1997, after he oversaw the transfer of Costinha, then a Portuguese second-division player, to Monaco. Costinha helped Monaco triumph and become champions of Ligue 1, before going on to win both the UEFA Cup and the Champions League as part of José Mourinho's Porto side – defeating Monaco in the latter final.

Since Rybolovlev has taken over the reins of the club, the relationship between club and agent has become increasingly high-profile, giving rise to jealousy and questioning. Mendes remains unperturbed. On 2 August 2015, Mendes married lawyer Sandra Barbosa in Porto. Their wedding was a lavish, high-society affair, with more than 400 guests gathering at the Serralves Foundation to watch the happy couple say their 'I do's'. Among the crowd of well-wishers was, of course, Cristiano Ronaldo, who presented his agent with a Greek island as a wedding gift. Other famous faces included the leaders of Real Madrid, Chelsea, Valencia, and PSG, along with the former boss of Barcelona. Rybolovlev was invited, but didn't attend. However, the Monaco clan weren't absent – Vasilyev, a long-time friend of Mendes, was in attendance. Luis Campos, the club's then technical director, was also invited.

The Porto wedding was an opportunity for Vasilyev and Campos to discuss a decision that had shaken the club. A few days earlier, the Portuguese director, who watched all matches from the bench ordinarily, had handed in his letter of resignation. It was rumoured that Campos was tired of being restricted in his scouting – something that was rather hard to stomach for a serious networker. Two days after Mendes's wedding, as Monaco were preparing for an important Champions League qualifier against the Swiss club BSC Young Boys, a solution to Campos's resignation was found. Monaco accepted Campos's resignation, but he was to stay on at the club as a 'special advisor to the vice president in a role with an international emphasis, focusing on recruitment and the detection of future talent'. Vasilyev was once again responsible for the daily management of the sports department.

Among the five football 'saviours' mentioned by Jorge Mendes, two of which play in Ligue 1. This is no coincidence, given that Dmitry Rybolovlev and Nasser Al-Khelaifi both belong to the new power set. They are de facto associates, as their finances have been unaffected by the post-2008 financial crisis.

Apart from ambition, the two club leaders don't have much in common. Nasser Al-Khelaifi loves to be photographed, always has a broad smile, participates in every press conference for 'galactic' recruits, gives interviews in French, and has been transformed into an outstanding ambassador and asset for his oft-criticised, native Qatar. For example, he was invited to Nicolas Sarkozy's sixtieth birthday, at his home in the 16th arrondissement of Paris.

Al-Khelaifi comes from a line of pearl fishermen, but he is also a former professional tennis player and trusted right-hand man to Sheikh Tamim al-Thani, Emir of Qatar. At only forty-three, he is the chairman of Qatar Sports Investments, the sovereign wealth fund that owns, among other assets, PSG and beIN Media Group (formerly Al-Jazeera Sport), of which beIN Sports France is one of its subsidiaries. The only official meetings Al-Khelaifi has had with Rybolovlev have taken place during championship matches between the two clubs in Paris, while Vasilyev was also present. However, on

22 September 2013, at the Parc des Princes, they found themselves face to face, separated only by the former French head of state Nicolas Sarkozy.

It was Rybolovlev's first visit to the stadium as chairman of Monaco, with the game ending in a one-all draw: Zlatan Ibrahimović scored the opening goal in the fifth minute, with Falcao equalising fifteen minutes later. In a rare gesture for an adversary, Rybolovlev was offered a lounge entirely for the use of his guests.

'Everyone wanted to meet him and try to unravel the mystery,' recalls Bruno Skropeta, head of communication at ASM and, since November 2015, also head of marketing. 'At half-time, a meeting was organised with Nicolas Sarkozy, an avid football fan and supporter of PSG. He thanked Rybolovlev for bringing added competition and quality players into the championship.'[79]

But even if one day (letting our imagination run a bit wild here) Rybolovlev was to open up to the press in French, in the way that Nasser al-Khelaifi, who, since QSI arrived in June 2011, has already won more than ten trophies, he is not in the seduction phase. It's just not his style.

He's someone that stays in the background. He has never been one for pomp and ceremony, and prefers to rely on his inner circle. He's a discreet character, calm and thoughtful.

---

79   Interview with the author.

In contrast to the likes of Jean-Michel Aulas, he's not the sales rep for the club! While the president of PSG is more often in the celebrity world, neither of them lack respect for institutions,[80]

summarises the sports economy expert Wulfran Devauchelle.

According to Devauchelle, Rybolovlev cannot be compared to other Russians who have invested in football, such as Abramovich and Alisher Usmanov, one of the main shareholders in Arsenal. 'The timing isn't the same, because the introduction of [UEFA] Financial Fair Play [Regulations], which came into force in 2011, changed the rules and had a negative impact on investors. In a way, Rybolovlev came onto the scene too late!' says Devauchelle.

But it certainly wasn't too late for Jean-Raymond Legrand – chairman of Valenciennes from 2011 to 2014 and proud to have been one of the first directors in Ligue 1 to negotiate with the billionaire. The case in question concerned centre-back Nicolas Isimat-Mirin.

'He met me in his Monaco apartment, with his lawyer present as a translator. I could see that he was a man of his word,' recalls Legrand.

The discussion was friendly and he told me, 'OK, we'll take your player.' It was May, and I had one requirement: that the

---

80   Interview with the author.

transfer would be completed before 30 June 2013, so that the transaction would be entered into the accounts and balance the books. But the deal dragged on. I started to lose my patience because we weren't making any progress.[81] On 30 June, he called me, and Vadim Vasilyev was also on the line, and he arranged for the commitment to be respected.[82]

And that is how 21-year-old Nicolas Isimat-Mirin came to sign a four-year contract with ASM – bringing Valenciennes a €4 million boost in funds. The defender never really made his mark in Monaco, though, and was loaned out to PSV Eindhoven the following season, where he helped his team win the Dutch title, prompting PSV to purchase the young player. His unsuccessful spell at Monaco didn't change the good relationship between Legrand and Rybolovlev.

Born to a miner father and housewife mother, Legrand is an autodidact who became an entrepreneur, with his business interests spanning waste recycling to an industrial bakery and from dealing in scrap iron to the hospitality industry.

Rybolovlev is clear, transparent, straightforward and honest. If he has money, he invests it in football carefully, making sure he is informed appropriately. He also has a surprising

---

81   The transfer was blocked following the judicial and media battle between the League and Monaco.
82   Interview with the author.

deadpan humour, and he really loves France. Contrary to appearances, he enjoys contact with people. I'm an underling, and yet he welcomed me with the utmost courtesy.

says Legrand. 'I know I'm welcome in Monaco, and that's a nice feeling. All club presidents are competitors first and foremost, but, with him, the relationship is professional and rather friendly. In France, we like to criticise people's accomplishments. He's rich and successful; I can only congratulate him!'

Legrand, who invested €13.6 million of his own money in Valenciennes and who is still a 15 per cent shareholder, has just one regret: unable to attend due to unavoidable obligations, Rybolovlev wasn't present at ASM's victory at the Stade du Hainaut in May 2014, as the Valenciennes team were relegated to Ligue 2, and Legrand was getting ready to hand over the reins.

This goodwill towards Rybolovlev is less marked at Olympique de Marseille, despite Vasilyev getting on well with his fellow Russian national Margarita Louis-Dreyfus, the club's majority shareholder until summer 2016. And so, when Monaco had once again joined the elite, Vincent Labrune, head of Marseille, shot straight from the hip in May 2013 with his words in *Le Parisien*:

A foreign club has arrived in League 1. Let me welcome ASM; you deserve your place in L1. But, this transition needs to

happen with all due respect to the law and the legal and eth-
ical regulations defined by the LFP. It's not a question of a
fight, it's just about fairness.

Marseille was one of the most determined French clubs
when it came to forcing Monaco to have its headquarters
in French territory, and therefore to be subject to the same
rules as other French clubs. Labrune's wrath was even more
virulent, as the 75 per cent tax rate – applied to Ligue 1 clubs
employing players whose income was above €1 million per
year – had just come into force. This was a tax for which
Monaco was exempt due to its tax domicile, not to mention
the fact that non-French nationals there do not pay income
tax at all.[83]

Thus, although the two clubs had a near identical budget
in the summer of 2013, Monaco was able to pay a €10 million
annual salary to Falcao, without any charges, while Marseille
was severely affected by supplementary taxation for its millionaire players. A few months later, two days before Paris
St-Germain were to visit the Vélodrome, Labrune was asked
if PSG vs. Monaco was in the process of becoming the new
classic confrontation of the championship. This time he took
a humorous approach:

I would call PSG vs. Monaco more of an 'hors taxico' [tax

---

free] combat! No, I'm just kidding. There's only one Clásico – Paris vs. Marseille – and that won't change. But it is true that if expenses continue to be systematically increased, it will become more and more complicated for a club like Marseille to be competitive against Paris and Monaco.

But Labrune also knows when to turn to pragmatism, if it's a question of closing a deal. He wasn't unhappy when Ocampos went on loan from Monaco to Marseille on the last day of the winter transfer window. In June 2015, Marseille even took up the purchase option for the 21-year-old midfielder at €7 million for a player prospected from Argentinian club River Plate three years earlier by ASM for €11 million. For his part, Aulas, chairman of Olympique Lyonnais, also gave up two jewels from his training centre to Monaco. On 30 June 2013, forward Anthony Martial arrived at Monaco, in exchange for €5 million (plus a prescient profit-sharing scheme of 20 per cent on future transfers and the five per cent solidarity tax for training). It was a remarkable sum for a seventeen-year-old player, certainly a precocious talent, but with only three Ligue 1 matches under his belt. It was a way of replenishing funds for Olympique Lyonnais, which, in its own words 'had to carry out a transfer before the end of the 2012–13 season in order to achieve its financial strategy.'

The sell-on clause proved wise. In September 2015, Martial, now with fifty-two Ligue 1 matches to his name, but still uncapped, was called up by the French national team. He was promptly given authorisation to leave the French training camp and sign with Manchester United for the incredible sum of €50 million, with his contract including three bonus clauses, bringing the potential total to €80 million. The first bonus was triggered in April 2017 when he scored his twenty-fifth senior goal for Manchester United. The second will come if, and when, he reaches twenty-five caps for France (he won his fifteenth in October 2016), and the third if he is nominated for the Ballon d'Or before 2019.

Should all the bonuses be activated, Martial would became the most expensive French player of all time, eclipsing the record set when Real Madrid purchased Zinedine Zidane from Juventus for €75 million in 2001. Zidane's former national captain and now France coach, Didier Deschamps, said: 'He's going to a very big club; he's changing planets and even galaxies. It's up to him to continue to progress and earn time on the field.'

Martial was a significant loss on a sporting level, especially as he wasn't immediately replaced – Rybolovlev hadn't wanted to rush into anything, given that Martial's move was announced on the last day of the transfer window – but the sale of Martial generated a huge profit, even with €10–€16 million having to be passed on to Lyon. Nevertheless, Vasilyev felt he needed to state on the ASM website that:

Transfers are part of football economics. Apart from the ten biggest clubs in the world, no one can buy without selling, and we are no different. Over the course of this summer, we have invested nearly €75 million across eleven players. All our actions are jointly decided with the technical staff. For Martial, it was different. We really wanted to keep him, but Manchester [United] made an incredible offer right at the end of the transfer window, and neither the club nor the player could refuse ... When our players leave us for Manchester United, Atletico Madrid, Valencia, PSG or Inter Milan, we know it's difficult to fight, but in a way, we can be proud of the work we've done, because our members join world-renowned clubs. Of course, I would like to keep them for longer, but you have to be realistic given the power of these clubs.

On 30 August, the day before the transfer was confirmed, United had proposed €50 million, ASM hadn't agreed. But when Vasilyev told Rybolovlev of the final sum that Manchester were willing to pay, Rybolovlev gave the green light personally. And with no qualms either, because Rybolovlev believed that economic logic would always win out over sporting logic. But another, last-minute offer was made at the end of that surreal transfer window: caught up in the transfer frenzy, Chelsea had made an even higher bid for the up-and-coming player, but Monaco had given its word to the Red Devils.

Prospecting is not an exact science, as much as Monaco try to make it one. Two years to the day of Monaco having signed Martial, Monaco acquired another prospect for €3 million, again from Lyon, in the form of twenty-year-old attacking midfielder Farès Bahlouli. However, although he was regarded as technically outstanding, he made only eight appearances for Monaco before being loaned to Belgium team Standard Liège, after which he was sold to Lille for the same €3 million.

Neither Martial's success nor Bahlouli's failure affected the good relationship between Rybolovlev and Aulas, Lyon's shrewd owner/president. The businessman, who founded his first company at the age of nineteen, made his fortune with Cegid – a provider of management software for chartered accountants. He took the helm at Lyon in 1987, taking the club from Ligue 2 to seven consecutive French championship titles from 2002 to 2008. He was very close to Jean-Louis Campora, the former Monaco president, and though his friendship with Rybolovlev is more subdued, it nevertheless exists.

Before making a judgement about Rybolovlev's character, Aulas insisted on getting to know the Monaco boss. He invited him to the Stade Gerland in February 2013 to watch the Europa League match between Lyon and Tottenham.

Aulas recalls:

Michel Platini (ex-French captain, former president of UEFA) had already spoken with him, and let me know that he knew a lot about football. He was the investor behind

Monaco, so naturally I met with him, just as I did when Nasser Al-Khelaifi took over at PSG. But, it was by conviction rather than strategy – it's always preferable to be on good terms with those two! I used to be president of the G-14,[84] and I still think it's important to understand the added value of anything within the realms of my own interests and the milieu in which I continue to evolve.

I could see that Dmitry Rybolovlev was a man that thinks before he acts, which is not always the case in football. You can immediately tell when someone is an imposing figure – and it's not just because of their bodyguard. He continually thinks and listens. In a public place, he is aware of everything, watches everything. He speaks rarely, but always with due consideration. He is discreet, not detached. I could see that he was aware of European models and rules, from televised rights to financial fair play. He undeniably has charisma. And he has an entrepreneurial spirit; he's someone that has succeeded in life, has built an empire. I didn't get to see a more private side, but I got to know a positive, engaging personality, with infinite power. You can sense his incredible strength of character. He is the master of his own destiny; a Napoleonic destiny. He obviously has moments of self-doubt and fear, but he doesn't let them show. Also, he has an effective secular

---

84   Today disbanded, this lobbying group based in Brussels grouped together fourteen, then eighteen of the most influential clubs in Europe. It was replaced in 2008 by the European Club Association (ECA), of which Aulas is board member, chairman of the Finance Working Group, and chairman of the Women's Football Committee. The ECA has 214 members from fifty-three associations.

muscle in the form of Vadim Vasilyev, with whom I've built up a relationship based on respect. They complement each other perfectly, and Vadim implements the club's strategy, which the boss decides upon.[85]

The two chairmen are also neighbours, both owning properties in Saint-Tropez. Rybolovlev was pleased to be able to show Aulas around his home. 'He has totally renovated it and it's one of the most beautiful [houses] in Saint-Tropez,' confirmed the head of Lyon.

This kind of meeting allows professional relationships to mature. He doesn't purposely create a distance the way Roman Abramovich is apt to do. Instead, he reminds me of leaders of clubs in Eastern European countries, industrialists who hold all the power, like, for example, at Shakhtar Donetsk in the Ukraine.[86]

They also like to dine together at Bagatelle, a hip, French bistro chain owned by Aymeric Clemente and Remi Laba. Its first restaurant opened in New York in 2007. The Bagatelle restaurants are always full and, thanks to the financial support of the Russian billionaire, the brand has spread from the US to Dubai and from São Paulo to the beach at

---

85 Interview with the author.
86 Since 1996, the chairman of this Ukrainian football club has been billionaire and politician Rinat Akhmetov. Under his reign, Shakhtar has secured ten championship titles and ten Ukraine Cups as well as the UEFA Cup.

Saint-Tropez, via Miami, Barcelona, and Monaco. But what really amazes Aulas is the low rate of recruitment error:

> Monaco never makes a mistake when buying players. They have tremendous expertise, a large database, and also often work through agent Jorge Mendes, which I'm not so happy about. They managed to sell James Rodríguez for €80 million to Real Madrid, Yannick Ferreira Carrasco for €20 million to Atletico Madrid and Geoffrey Kondogbia to Inter Milan at the same price that we released Michael Essien to Chelsea in 2005 (€38 million).[87] Lyon's days of glory have been beaten hands down! Their transfer market is impressive. Now we have to wait and see what they will do with all their millions. I am very keen to find out the rest of the story.

'In the football world, Saint-Étienne will always be the capital and Lyon its suburbs,' Roger Rocher had claimed. The man with the pipe, chairman of Les Verts (AS Saint-Étienne) for twenty years, during which time his club won title after title: they were nine times champion of France, the winners of six Coupes de France and even had a parade in their honour down the Champs-Élysées in 1976, after being defeated by Bayern Munich in the final of the European Cup, due to those damned 'poteaux carrés' ('square posts', the supporters' nickname for the goalposts)!

---

87 The interview took place before Anthony Martial's transfer, sold by Monaco to Manchester United in late August 2015.

Since then, Lyon have overtaken their neighbour. But their hotly contested derbies are still fairly evenly balanced. Anything can happen. On the subject of Rybolovlev, Bernard Caïazzo, president of the supervisory board of AS Saint-Étienne, is of the same opinion as Aulas. The same Caïazzo that invited Rybolovlev to the 'Cauldron', or Geoffroy-Guichard Stadium on 1 March 2014, when the team from Saint-Étienne beat Monaco 2–1 – the first team that year to do so. Despite the result, the defeated party flew Caïazzo home to the south of France; he divides his time normally between his residences near Cannes, Paris, and Saint-Étienne. 'I have never done business with them; there haven't been any transfers between the two clubs since he arrived,' says Caïazzo,[88] 'but ASSE has a strong relationship with Monaco, which allows us to judge people without taking financial interests into account.'

We're rivals on the field, we have created a partnership to develop French football, and I haven't forgotten that, based on the UEFA coefficient, we have gained advantage over Russian clubs thanks to Monaco's performances in the Champions League. And with a right-hand man whose human relationships are as impeccable as Vasilyev's are, Rybolovlev is surrounded by the right people. He's the strict father, while the emotional side of the household is managed by the mother,

---

88   This was the case until 31 July 2015, when winger Alan Saint-Maximin, eighteen years old and after nine championship matches with Les Verts the previous season, signed up for five years with Monaco, who immediately lent him to Hanover, Germany.

the vice president. He is intelligent enough to delegate aspects he is not familiar with to people better qualified than him. Their alliance is clear-sighted and the tasks well allocated.

Also, he's not in a position where he needs to ask favours, which encourages a positive atmosphere. He is neither arrogant, nor, as it could be said, has he emerged from the oligarch system: he made his fortune through hard work and not in a deceitful way by plundering the Russian people. Given all the problems with the League, Federation, Financial Fair Play, and unfulfilled promises, Rybolovlev could have felt rejected and said: 'I don't need you; I'll put my money elsewhere.' But there was no way he was going to be the sucker that people took advantage of! That certainly didn't happen, and Monaco has cleverly adapted by recruiting lots of young players.[89]

But Caïazzo hasn't always been so indulgent towards the Russian. As ASM started climbing up the League ranks, without most of the club presidents realising, Caïazzo, in his role as vice president of the UCPF (the French Union for Professional Clubs), gave an initial alert regarding Monaco's exemption from the 75 per cent tax rate. And after a stormy meeting in May 2013 with Noël Le Graët, chairman of the French Federation, who sought €200 million from Rybolovlev as a form of compensation for the Monegasque taxation advantages, Caïazzo once again bared his claws in

---

89   Interview with the author.

France Football: 'Apparently during the interview, he started to become insulting. That shows an unacceptable lack of respect. If it's true, it would be good if Rybolovlev apologised to Noël Le Graët. A moment of irritation is understandable, but afterwards, apologies have to be made.'

That was how Caïazzo saw things at the time. He explains: 'In the beginning, it's true that there was a kind of generalised movement among the clubs. It wasn't against him directly, but was connected to Monegasque taxation, which results in a substantial imbalance regarding expenses,' he says.

> When Monaco recruits a big star the dice are loaded and it's not fair. The amount requested in compensation seemed reasonable to me, allowing us to get back on our feet. It was better to reach a poor deal than go through a long court case! I thought about it a lot and discussed it with them, because it didn't seem worthwhile fighting against things you can't prevent.
>
> In terms of the stadium and sponsoring revenue, Monaco is at a considerable disadvantage. Let me put it this way, that shortfall could be seen as a kind of penalty when it comes to buying players. It was a question of being objective and being aware of that reality. But it was never a question of ASM not participating in the French championship. No one would have accepted that, least of all the state.

In the end, even the €50 million Monaco agreed to pay was deemed 'illegal' by the courts, to the disappointment of Bordeaux president Jean-Louis Triaud, who was heavily involved in the case.

> I don't know Rybolovlev and I have nothing against him. I have only crossed paths with him once, and we acknowledged one another. But it's a question of principles. Since I have been in football [Triaud has been head of the Girondins since 1996] and on the league's board of administrators, I have always strongly opposed the exorbitant advantages that the club benefits from, even at the time of Campora

he says, hammering the point home.

> Their status is irregular, and their team should have the same constraints that we do, by shifting its headquarters to France and dealing with an identical tax system. It's as if, in a 100m race, you start one athlete ten metres ahead of the others. I don't want any money in compensation, I would just like for us all to be competing in the same championship. The rules have not been respected and there is a growing feeling that a new rule has been invented especially for Monaco.[90]

An extraordinary person and the most senior president in Ligue 1 (he has been head of Montpellier Herault since 1974), Louis Nicollin also belongs to the camp opposed to Monaco.

---

90   Interview with the author.

The president of the 2012 French champions swears that, once again, the disagreement isn't personal. 'Not only do I bear no ill-will towards the Russians, but my friend Gérard Depardieu is great friends with Vladimir Putin!' laughs Loulou.

> Our total budget is €50 million; it's just ridiculous. There should be a level playing field from the outset; that's why it seemed fair to me that Monaco pay the same expenses, and this is without taking into account the fact that they already have an advantage, as foreign high-income salaries don't pay tax. I didn't give a damn about the few thousand euros they agreed to put into the overall kitty!
>
> Even though their status is far from new, I can remember when Jean-Louis Campora and I were vice presidents of the League, the mindset was different. And what would happen if Montpellier set up its headquarters in Andorra? But, I do agree that PSG and Monaco raise the level of the game, and that people outside of France are starting to talk about the championship. I was on holiday in Mauritius, and for the first time, someone asked me about Ligue 2!

The president of Montpellier is a successful businessman himself. Since 1977, he has transformed the business established after the war by his father, Marcel, which specialises in cleaning and waste collection. It is now the third-biggest waste management company in the country with 5,000 employees and a €300 million turnover. He is not envious of the Russian billionaire's fortune:

> He does what he likes with his money. I won't say anything bad about him; I don't know him at all. But I have been invited to Vadim Vasilyev's box. He was polite and seemed to be a nice guy. Being part of this world, I've come across some club presidents who were arrogant and acted like idiots, but in the box in Monaco ... well, I was mostly looking at the pretty girls, anyway.

CHAPTER 11

PLEASURES OF A BILLIONAIRE

Lottery winners know what it feels like. That strange sensation when you hit the jackpot with a stroke of unimaginable good luck, leading to a timeless moment that is both euphoric and disturbing. Immense joy; tangible happiness that materialises when you travel around the world or buy a new racing car. But this is often followed by the need to decompress or a sense of dismay, or, for some, even depression. Some winners have ended up ruined by a neighbour, a dishonest family member, or simply their inability to handle their new-found riches. It's different for those born into wealth, but the majority of us simply can't learn or be taught how to cope with becoming incredibly wealthy overnight. Many national lotteries, including those of England and France, provide support to winners to assist and guide them. There are even support groups with therapists, as lottery boards are aware of how unprepared most winners are and how fleeting their new-found wealth may be.

Dmitry Rybolovlev didn't become a billionaire by

randomly ticking numbered boxes. He built up his fortune methodically. But his forced exit from Uralkali in the
summer of 2010 was when he really struck gold. Rybolovlev
was forced to sell his shares in the giant potassium company
that he had transformed, and when his virtual funds became
concrete, he was left with an outrageous sum of money – he
now had more than €5 billion in the bank.

Once they have gotten over the understandable desire to
spend wildly, most jackpot winners will use their money to
buy a new house or place it in secure investments. Rybolovlev's situation was different. Even though he hadn't been born
into a wealthy family, he had had the time to adjust to a life of
luxury. Before leaving Uralkali, he had already had a taste of
the high life. But rather than frittering away his fortune after
having been 'freed' from his potassium obligations, his first
concern was filling the void that leaving his company behind
had left. Keep busy. Find something stimulating to work
on – which doesn't necessarily mean not enjoying yourself.
His life had been an endless tunnel since his seven years of
medical study, followed by his financial apprenticeship in
Moscow and the wild privatisation adventure in the form of
Uralkali. He was yearning to take a break.

'I didn't immediately find an interesting business proposition, so I travelled the world,'[91] he says. He adds, 'I had been
so focused on my business that I really needed to disconnect

---

from it. I made the most of life! But not for long. I can't just do nothing. I need to be right amongst the action.'

Before getting involved in business once again and moving to Monaco in 2011, Rybolovlev got some good use out of his amazing 'toys', made possible by his extensive property portfolio. Some of the items bought via family trusts included masterpieces by Van Gogh, Picasso, Gauguin, and Monet; two aeroplanes, together worth approximately €80 million (an Airbus A319 and a Dassault Falcon 7X trijet with a range of 11,000 km, since sold); a 67-metre yacht; a villa in Hawaii; a private mansion in Paris on Rue de l'Élysée; two luxury chalets in Gstaad, Switzerland; an apartment in Hotel Moskva overlooking the Red Square; and the Voentorg shopping centre in Moscow. At this point in his life, it was enough to be able to devote himself to his passion for surfing and jet-ski, to visit museums (with a preference for post-impressionists), attend the opera and ballet, go to classical music concerts, and applaud the entrechats, or leaps, of the Bolshoi prima ballerina Svetlana Zakharova at La Scala in Milan.

In 2008, Rybolovlev used the family trust to buy the Maison de l'Amitié, a luxurious property on the Florida waterfront in Palm Beach featuring a ballroom, eighteen bedrooms, and a gigantic swimming pool amid 80,000m² of land. It was on the market for $95 million cash, but more notable than the hefty price tag was the seller. Then just a real estate mogul with an overdeveloped ego, Donald Trump would shock the world eight years later by becoming President of the United States.

President Trump was immediately embroiled in allegations concerning Russian influence on his election win. This inevitably led to rumours and, in early 2017, parts of the US blogosphere made claims that Rybolovlev was some kind of secret Russian envoy to Trump, despite both parties insisting that the two men have never actually met – at this level vendors tend not to show prospective house buyers around themselves. It soon became clear that there was no substance behind the speculation, and Rybolovlev's name dropped back off the political radar, resurfacing briefly when he knocked down Maison de l'Amitié, divided the land into three plots, and began selling the plots individually. The first lot went for $34.34 million in 2017.

The property had been purchased through the family trust established in 2005 in Cyprus, of which he and his children are beneficiaries. The same trust provided the necessary funds for another splurge in late 2011, which this time was an apartment in New York, which he bought for his daughter Ekaterina. The apartment was sold for $88 million, which at the time was the record for an individual residence in the Big Apple. But not for long; in July 2012, a 1,020m² penthouse split across the top stories of the One57 skyscraper went for $100 million. Rumour had it that they were purchased by the Prime Minister of Qatar. Rybolovlev had been beaten by PSG once again.

His daughter's prized possession (627m² for ten rooms, and a 186m² terrace) is right on the prestigious 15 Central Park West and overlooks Manhattan's immense green space. At the time, Ekaterina was taking classes in psychology and finance at Harvard by correspondence. The price really got people talking, as it eclipsed the previous highest paid price for a New York property by $35 million – set by a former partner at Goldman Sachs four years prior. The apartment acquired by Ekaterina had previously belonged to the director of Citigroup bank.

Rybolovlev is willing to do anything for his daughters – the apples of his eye. Anna, the youngest, of whom no photos exist publicly, was born in 2001 in Geneva. She is a cheerful, energetic, and athletic girl who is passionate about drawing and music – she plays the piano. She lives with her mother in Switzerland. The eldest, blonde Ekaterina, whom everyone calls Katia (no doubt so as not to have the same initials as her mother), was born in Perm in June 1989. With her pale skin and reserved personality, she resembles her father. She grew up in Russia, before accompanying her parents to the shores of Lake Geneva. At a young age, she began riding classes and started competing in equestrian events. She owns several horses – Uropo, Cherubin van de Helle, Lucky the Man, Obelix du Thot, Celesto Z, and Eole Perruques – which she rides in competitions.

In 2008, Ekaterina (who has studied at Cambridge) won an event at a dressage competition in Geneva on her mare

Eole. Trained by Englishman Ben Maher, a three-time Olympian and team gold medallist at London 2012, she has competed at the Gucci Masters and the Show Jumping World Cup. Being part of the equestrian world allowed her to meet Athina Onassis-Roussel, Aristotle's granddaughter and the only surviving heir to the family empire built up by the shipping magnate. This led to the purchase of the Greek island of Skorpios in 2013.

Widely travelled, she divides her time between Monaco, New York, and London. She is a member of the board of administrators of AS Monaco, and while she is only involved to a certain degree with the club, when it was in Ligue 2, she sometimes represented her father at meetings, making the final decision in some cases. She also had some involvement in Uralkali and collaborates with an American investment bank.

Naturally discreet, the equestrian agreed to a short interview with *Paris Match* in November 2013. It afforded the opportunity to describe the relationship she has with her father, which the magazine devoted eight pages to. 'Our father–daughter relationship is excellent, but things can get heated as soon as we talk about business,' she said. 'We both have strong characters. The apple never falls far from the tree.'

Ekaterina also shared how their relationship has developed:

> As a young child I lived in Switzerland with my mother. My father was occupied with his business, and I didn't see him

often. Then, like everyone, I had my teenage crisis and I often disagreed with my mother, but my father helped me a lot. The divorce brought us even closer together. He is very present in my life ... and very demanding.

That demanding nature has occasionally been seen at ASM, though Rybolovlev is not the sort of chairman to scream at his coaches. His anger is colder. 'In ten years of collaboration – seven at Uralkali and three at Monaco at the club and the family office – I have only really seen him get angry and beside himself two or three times', says Dmitry Chechkin, former vice president of ASM.

Usually, he has complete control of himself and shows no emotion. He doesn't have any particular need to display his power. Often on the first meeting, he comes across as a cold and closed man. At the same time, he can be very pleasant to talk to. But actually, he is only natural and truly himself when he is with his parents, children and closest friends.[92]

One occasion on which the chairman made clear his dissatisfaction to his players and coach was after a bitter 3–0 setback in Angers. The following week he burst into the changing room (a rare event) before the kick-off against Bastia. Jardim explains it as follows:

---

92   Interview with the author.

It's not a question of putting the pressure on. But, well, he had seen the team's poor form at the last match. It was sad, and he came to motivate the team. We had performed better, even if we had already won four victories out of the last five matches. It proves that he is present: for players, for staff, for everybody.

The following Thursday, he was at the training centre La Turbie, with sunglasses and a club jacket over his shoulders, watching the session and exchanging a few words with Jardim.

His appearances at La Turbie are infrequent. 'At first, perhaps, he can be intimidating for players, because he likes to observe,' smiles Bruno Skropeta, head of communication and marketing.

But once they have had the chance to talk with the chairman, the players get to know him and recognise his passion for football. He has come to watch training sessions several times, once even very early on a Saturday morning for a match between starting players and substitutes, during an international break. He was seated on a small chair next to the bench.[93]

On that particular day in October 2013, the Danish international midfielder Jakob Poulsen, who has often played as a

---

93   Interview with the author.

substitute since the team's promotion to Ligue 1, performed an amazing shot. From the touch line, he sent a ball directly into a string bag holding all the balls, tens of metres away and held by Fabinho. It was a precise and spectacular shot that did the rounds on the Internet.

'Rybolovlev appreciates the opportunity to talk with players and understand their psychology,' adds Skropeta, who was also part of a friendly five-a-side at La Turbie in March 2016 when Rybolovlev joined in with coach Leonardo Jardim, technical director Claude Makelele (the former France, Chelsea, and Real Madrid midfielder), and other staff members. The game finished 3–3, though history doesn't tell us whether the chairman scored.

The Russian was, however, able to rejoice two days later when AS Monaco triumphed at the Parc des Princes against the already-crowned champions of France, Paris Saint-Germain (2–0). That prestigious victory consolidated second place, qualifying Monaco for the Champions League. In the euphoria of the moment, Rybolovlev congratulated his players, telling them how proud he was of the image they portrayed.

Rybolovlev is very much a fan. Present at almost all matches at Louis-II, he is transported by the merest whiff of the Champions League; a photo of the leap he made from his seat with fists clenched, alongside Prince Albert and league president Frédéric Thiriez, as Moutinho scored the winning goal against Bayer Leverkusen, adorns the desk of Filips Dhondt, Vasilyev's advisor.

Irina Petrovna Koryukina, director of the Medical Academy at Perm, where he studied and where his parents taught for a long time, has seen his enthusiasm first-hand. Her eldest son, Alexandre, is fourteen years old and loves football, playing at a promising level. The billionaire invited her and Alexandre to watch a training session at La Turbie, followed by a match. 'We were in the box with him. It was interesting to watch,' recalls Koryukina. 'Dmitry was focused on the match and was impassive. And then, when his team scored, he jumped right up. He was like a child ... His face totally lit up with happiness.'[94]

Rybolovlev enjoys having guests at Stade Louis II, hosting several VIP invitees, other Monaco citizens at heart, such as long-time world tennis No. 1 Novak Djokovic and three-time Formula 1 world champion Lewis Hamilton, who live on the Rock; comedian Gad Elmaleh, who has a son with Charlotte Casiraghi, member of the Prince's family; or U2 singer Bono, who lives nearby for part of the year, at Èze. One absentee was François Hollande, despite the former President of the French republic once confessing that, while known as a Red Star Paris fan, his childhood favourite was Monaco.[95]

Hollande's successor is unlikely to appear either. The

---

94 Interview with the author.
95 When in January 2012, France Football asked him if it was true that his favourite club was Monaco, Hollande replied, 'Yes, for a while, it was Monaco. At one point they had a great team! With Trezeguet and Henry ... But I'm talking about the Monaco I would go to watch, with Wenger as coach, Thuram, Ettori, Klinsmann, Hoddle.'

fly-on-the-wall television film *Macron: Behind the Scenes of a Victory*, which revealed the inside story of the 2017 election winner's campaign, included a scene in which Macron swears: 'Oh s***, for the second time... F***,' he says. His wife Brigitte asks him what is wrong, only for him to explain: 'Monaco has defeated Marseille, in Marseille.' Brigitte is uninterested in the revelation.

More likely guests would be the scientists behind the Human Brain Project, a landmark research programme costing €1 billion over ten years and largely funded by the European Union. Since 2013, Rybolovlev has attentively followed the project driven by Henry Markram at the École Polytechnique Fédérale de Lausanne (the Swiss Federal Institute of Technology in Lausanne), meeting the neuroscientist and his team. The project involves mapping the entire brain with the help of supercomputers, so that its mysteries, with its 100,000 billion synapses, will one day be revealed.

Markram, born in South Africa and a naturalised Israeli, described the benefits of this tool in the *Journal du Dimanche*:

Testing ideas and providing clues on where to look for new targets. At the moment, it takes thirteen years and billions of euros to develop medicine to combat Alzheimer's or Parkinson's disease. With this model, we will be able to test all sorts of things, and then select one or two key hypotheses to experiment with.

This virtual laboratory with six platforms facilitates exchange between specialists, whether they are sociologists, neurologists, computer scientists, mathematicians, biologists, geneticists, or psychiatrists.

The Monegasque chairman, a qualified physician remember, is also aware of the efforts of the Institut du Cerveau et de la Moelle Épinière – the ICM (Brain and Spine Institute), which brings together scientists aiming to treat central nervous system lesions. A private foundation, the ICM is situated within the Hôpital de la Pitié-Salpêtrière, Paris. It is led by professor of orthopaedic surgery and traumatology Gérard Saillant, to whom Ronaldo dedicated his Ballon d'Or. Its vice president Jean Todt also heads the Fédération Internationale de l'Automobile. Rybolovlev has a warm relationship with the former boss of Ferrari, whom he sees each year at the Monaco Formula 1 Grand Prix. Questioned in March 2015 by *Nice-Matin* about his vision for the future, the Russian expressed his conviction that 'we will continue to witness the development of technological innovations in various domains. As a trained doctor, I believe strongly in new biotechnologies and pharmaceutical progress, which will not only allow us to discover new methods for treating different diseases, but will also revolutionise our daily life.'

Health is, understandably, a subject close to his heart, especially as he has himself experienced a few issues, from the time spent in a sanatorium in Perm while he was at school to the eleven months he spent in prison, where he suffered from severe throat inflammation and kidney stones. And let's not forget the benign tumour that was operated on in 2014. This confidential information was revealed by *L'Équipe* on 25 June of the same year; three small lines to announce the operation on a tumour by American surgeons in Santo Domingo, the capital of the Dominican Republic. His fragile state of health and his absence from the stadium during the weeks that followed, as well as the constant secrecy surrounding him, contributed to the rumour that he wouldn't stay on indefinitely at AS Monaco – something that he downplays. 'I feel happy here. Our objective hasn't changed: to become the champion of France, and – why not – even win the Champions League.'

CHAPTER 12

THE 'DIVORCE OF THE CENTURY'

Rybolovlev's youngest daughter, Anna, was born in 2001. It was one of the rare happy memories from the long years Dmitry Rybolovlev spent in Switzerland. He settled there in 1995 with his then wife Elena and their eldest daughter, Ekaterina, who was six at the time. Switzerland, bordered by Italy, France, Germany, Austria, and Liechtenstein, met the family's criteria of tranquillity and security. In Perm Rybolovlev's potash-extraction company was so coveted that he spent his life surrounded by bodyguards. In that respect, Switzerland was a haven; it offered peace and quiet, along with every possible comfort. The country also possesses the world's fourth-highest GDP per inhabitant.

The Rybolovlevs were granted a resident's permit, indispensable when purchasing a house, and settled in Cologny, a small municipality with a verdant landscape, favoured by the wealthy (particularly wealthy Russians). The municipality has breath-taking views of Lake Geneva and the Jura mountains, not to mention an attractive tax system. A lover of classical music, Elena took to her new environment immediately; she learned French rapidly and launched an art foundation. Dmitry's business interests meant that he was away from home frequently, and he didn't become part of the local community.

Even though he was rarely in Cologny, Rybolovlev was nevertheless, like the other 5,000 inhabitants of this El Dorado, considered a 'Colognote'.

The chic suburb has long attracted flamboyant personalities. The novelist Mary Shelley is said to have stayed at one of the town's manors in 1816, while writing the initial pages of her literary classic *Frankenstein*. But instead of monsters unleashed on the world by Dr Frankenstein, Rybolovlev's neighbours included the daughter of the President of Uzbekistan; the son of a former Lebanese Prime Minister; German Klaus Schwab, president of the World Economic Forum in Davos; petrol oligarch Gennady Timchenko (who had a tennis court built under his house); singer Nana Mouskouri; and former world ski champion Jean-Claude Killy.

In Cologny, Rybolovlev felt a little confined, despite his imposing mansion; he had had dreams of grandeur and his home didn't match his vision. So, between 2002 and 2004, he bought up areas of land surrounding his property, with a view to turning them into one large area, covering 10,000m². He hoped to build on the enlarged section nothing less than a replica of the Petit Trianon at Versailles – a castle inspired by Madame de Pompadour, which Louis XVI had given to Queen Marie-Antoinette as a gift.

The original, absolutely sublime, is surrounded by gardens and has four façades. For his extraordinary palace, Rybolov-lev envisaged an interior swimming pool and a pavilion for guests, all overlooking Lake Geneva. The work, the total cost of which was estimated at €70 million, was begun and diggers began excavating huge holes. It was enough to spark his neighbours' ire and protests from the public art society (now Patrimoine Suisse), which lodged complaints against the three-storey building whose lakeside façade was above the requisite sixteen metres and obstructed the view for other residents. In spite of appeals, the administrative courts ultimately agreed with Rybolovlev. But the atmosphere was less than harmonious. Rybolovlev now associates Switzerland with the tension over the house; the time he spent in prison in Perm while his family stayed in Cologny; the break-up of his marriage; and, finally, the dispute with Genevan art dealer Yves Bouvier. In short, this country with its twenty-six cantons was not for him. There are just too many negative associations.

The 'hole of Cologny', which has been abandoned since the beginning of Rybolovlev's divorce proceedings, is often cited as a blot on the local landscape. The worksite at Chemin Bellefontaine stopped in 2009 while the foundations were still being laid. 'With its fences and abandoned excavation works at the end of a secluded small street, the millionaires' belvedere looks out over Geneva. It's the only sign of the replica of the Petit Trianon that Dmitry Rybolovlev and his wife Elena hoped to build,' writes *Le Temps*. The Swiss media have had a field day. A Swiss journalist who has followed Rybolovlev's ups and downs, and who asked to remain anonymous says:

> [Due to] Potash being less sexy than oil, Rybolovlev was for a long time unknown here, especially as, in 1995, when he sought refuge in Switzerland after the Kremlin came back into power, his fortune had not yet reached one billion. Good reasons to stay below the radar, particularly as he is not a street performer. But he's not a bandit either, he doesn't come from the lower rungs – he had intended to pursue a career in medicine. The issue with his villa worksite on the most expensive hill in town had started to attract attention.[96][97]

Rybolovlev does not attempt to cover things up – he doesn't hide the fact that he was not the ideal husband. His yacht parties on the Mediterranean were popular. Unable to put up with and denouncing his presumed infidelities any longer, Elena filed for divorce and demanded half of his fortune, claiming that although she hadn't worked in a professional capacity since leaving university after their

---

96   In the USSR at the time of their union in 1987, there was no marriage or property contract. 'Joint ownership of acquired property' did not become effective until after their move to Switzerland, where this legal status was applied by default.

97   Interview with the author.

daughter was born, she had contributed to the construction of Rybolovlev's potassium empire. And so the couple tore themselves apart. A merciless legal battle began as soon as Elena told her husband that she was leaving him in 2008, with each party delivering blow after devastating blow.

'Even more so than prison, which in some way was a useful life experience, there is a dark period in my existence: my marriage and the divorce that ensued,' says Rybolovlev.

> It took me a long time to digest, particularly as our children were at the centre of the issue. I would never have thought that she would ask for divorce, especially during a period where I was under so much pressure at Uralkali. From an emotional point of view, it was a very difficult time – my world was turned upside down. At the time, I didn't understand, but now that day in December 2008 is etched on my memory. I saw it as a betrayal.[98]

To defend her interests, Elena called on a master of the courts Marc Bonnant, seventy-one years old, with a white mane and renowned oratory skills. An apostle of the imperfect tense in French, he was admitted to the bar in 1971.

Le Nouvel Observateur recounted in May 2015 that:

> Divorce, murder, bankruptcy … the baseness of those in

---

98   Interview with the author.

power has been the bread and butter of his legal firm for forty-four years. His tiny waiting room must certainly be one of the top VIP areas in Europe. Considered by his peers as a Mozart of the courtroom, the former head of the Geneva bar has defended Edmond Safra, Édouard Stern's family, the widow of Yasser Arafat, the head of the P2 lodge Licio Gelli and Boris Berezovsky.

The journalist, between two curls of smoke from a Marlboro red, describes the office where five volumes of an edition of *Confessions* by Saint Augustine share shelf space with a collection of photos by Helmut Newton.

The criminal lawyer also has his grey areas. The online information website Mediapart has asserted that he was the administrator for Balerton Marketing Limited, an offshore company that holds a Swiss bank account belonging to Jean-Marie Le Pen, founder of the Front National, via a trust based in the British Virgin Islands, and placed under the legal responsibility of Le Pen's butler, also treasurer of two financial associations. A deposit of €2.2 million is said to have been made into the trust's account, with €1.7 million deposited in the form of gold coins and ingots. In addition, the revelations emerging from the Panama Papers in April 2016 have shed light on the feverish activity of the 'Cicero of the Courts'. It appears that he is, or has been, director of at least 176 offshore companies registered with the Panama law firm Mossack Fonseca for some its various clients, such as

Ziad Takieddine and the nephew of South African President Jacob Zuma.

Bonnant met Elena Rybolovleva for the first time at a dinner, one of many that take place in Geneva. She opened up to him about Dmitry's proposition: to withdraw the interest generated from the totality of his companies from their marital status. She had refused. And, when the case was to go to the Swiss courts, she asked the Genevan lawyer to support her in her battle. She quickly accused her husband of reducing his financial exposure and engineering his own insolvency.

The case, which had its fair share of twists and turns, is complex, particularly when it came to assessing the amount of assets stashed away, as from 2005 Rybolovlev had placed nearly 90 per cent of his fortune in trusts. In the same year he created two trusts based in Cyprus – Aries and Virgo – whom he is the 'protector' of. [99] The beneficiaries of the two trust are his two daughters. Slowly but surely, he transferred his companies and shares to Aries and Virgo. Under the Swiss system of joint ownership of acquired property, he didn't need his wife's authorisation to carry out the transfers and thus divested himself of his assets in favour of these trusts. She contested this, arguing that he acted intentionally, three-and-a-half years before she asked for a divorce. She multiplied her efforts to bring him down, which resulted in

---

99   The person responsible for controlling assets placed in the trust, monitoring the management of trustees, and dismissing them if necessary.

provisional asset seizures in various places (Switzerland, the British Virgin Islands, London, Florida, Cyprus, and Singapore), even managing to legally freeze his assets in 2010. Rybolovlev retaliated and appealed to the federal court to remove the block. He chose Tetiana Bersheda as his defence lawyer, a Swiss lawyer of Ukrainian origin whose father, a former professor of economics, had been ambassador to Bern.

In early 2009, while the polyglot was working at a renowned lawyer's office in Geneva, she was contacted by a client looking for a Russian-speaking lawyer to help with difficult divorce proceedings. Although Bersheda specialises in international law and commercial litigation resolution, she nevertheless accepted the opportunity to represent Rybolovlev, and met with the man who would become her most important client. Rybolovlev places a great deal of trust in her, to such an extent that at only thirty-two years of age, she is now a member of leadership structures for a number of organisations connected with his family, including the board of directors for AS Monaco.

Before meeting Rybolovlev, Bersheda had never been involved with a divorce case. She was clear about this with Rybolovlev from the outset, saying that she hoped it would be the first and the last that she would handle. She recalls:

He replied that his divorce was more similar to a commercial case than a matrimonial one, given the issues at stake. Over the course of our meetings, he opened up to me, since in order to prepare for the case, I needed to learn about his life. And what a dramatic life he has led, it is so moving. I have an enormous amount of respect and affection for him. He trusted me despite my young age and I am grateful to him for that. He has become a friend.

With his divorce case, it was all about staying serene and this wasn't easy, in view of the lies and nasty remarks that were written. He wasn't a model husband, and he did commit some indiscretions, nobody has tried to deny that. But he did all he could to save his family and protect his children. He was ready to compromise straight away. But in light of her strategy and tactics, it was clear his ex-wife was making it a purely financial battle, choosing, for example, to start the divorce proceedings when the value of his companies' capital stocks was at their highest.

The opposing party spoke to the media a lot, which is what you do when you aren't able to convince the judges! We never asked for special treatment, simply that the law be enforced.[100]

Elena Rybolovleva was contacted but chose not to be interviewed. And while Bonnant often pours out his feelings rather convincingly to the media, for this book he chose not to, considering himself 'bound to act with restraint given

---

100   Interview with the author.

that the case is ongoing' and knowing that his client 'intends to make an appeal to the Federal Supreme Court'.[101]

Elena opens up to the media directly only sparingly. She has broken her silence just twice, on both occasions through the Swiss economics magazine *Bilan*. The first was in January 2014, where she went on the offensive:

> With hindsight, I can see that my integration into Swiss life perhaps dealt the death blow to our relationship. While I was taking on the Helvetian way of life, my husband refused to westernise. He never participated in the social or cultural life of the city. We were no longer part of the same world ... In contrast to my husband, I live simply and my feet are firmly on the ground...
>
> As a good Russian mother, I am very proud of my children and I think I can say that I have taught them real values, despite the privileged environment in which they live, which could make them lose their grip on reality.

It was undoubtedly a way of replying to her ex-husband's cutting remarks in *Paris Match* two months earlier: 'We got married at a very young age, at twenty, and little by little we grew apart. My life took off and my wife stayed on the tarmac ... I travelled a lot, and she preferred to stay in Geneva, not wanting to return to Russia. I probably should have asked

---

for a divorce earlier. But if I didn't, it's because for me family is sacred.'

With regard to his trusts, he explains that they were created much earlier 'to provide for our children's future. This was done to plan the most efficient succession. And what really takes the biscuit is that my wife is taking it out on our daughters, who are obliged to defend themselves against their mother in a number of legal proceedings.'

On 13 May 2014, after six years of proceedings and sudden reversals, the Geneva courts made a decision to include the assets transferred to the trusts prior to the divorce as part of the total assets to be divided at the time of the divorce.

The first judgment thus ordered Rybolovlev to pay his ex-wife just under half of his fortune. The exact amount he had to pay Elena totalled 4,020,555,987 Swiss francs, approximately £3.2 billion. It was such a large sum that the break-up of their marriage was christened 'the divorce of the century'. Swiss law recognised that while he claimed not to own anything under his own name, he nevertheless had authority over the trustees (trust administrators, sole legal owners) and that those assets had to be included as part of the total.

Moreover, Elena was awarded parental rights over their youngest daughter, as well as certain assets held in trusts: jewellery, works of art, and properties, including their home in Cologny. She spoke again to *Bilan*, declaring herself satisfied with the verdict:

I am particularly happy with the judgment, not so much for the victory that it has awarded me, but because justice has been carried out according to the law, and calmly, just as it would have been for any Swiss couple … My husband and I didn't have a cent when we got married, and together we built a family and a fortune. It is therefore fair and in accordance with the law that this fortune be fairly shared at the time of the divorce. I know that my case is exceptional due to the amount in question, but the ruling magistrate showed no hesitation when he gave his verdict.

I have no regrets: not for the years of love or for having brought an end to a marriage that had become destructive. However, I deplore the fact that my husband decided to use our children as a screen between me and him, as a way of avoiding having to pay his debt. This divorce is between just the two of us and I'd hoped that he would have the courage and dignity to face up to me, rather than hiding behind his daughters and trustees.

But she had no illusions; she knew her husband wouldn't leave it at that. He immediately appealed against the judgment before the Cour de Justice, with suspensive effect, arguing that Swiss matrimonial law should not apply to the trust assets, as they are in Cyprus. Thirteen months later, on 11 June 2015, the sum Elena was due to receive was reduced to just an eighth of the original. Abuse of process was not upheld. Elena no longer had the right to

4 billion Swiss francs; she was now left with 564 million (£453 million).

Why was there such a discrepancy? It wasn't a question of deciding whether to split the assets between the former spouses, but a question of the amount that should be split. Plainly speaking, should the sum be based on the value of the assets when they were transferred into the trusts in 2005 or their value at the time of the divorce? It's as 'simple' as that. If they split the money that was put into the trusts in 2005, they would each receive half of 1 billion Swiss francs. But if they were to take the value of the assets in 2014, they would be splitting 8 billion, as this figure includes the profit made by Uralkali between 2005 and 2014. The company was listed on the stock exchange the previous year.

Inevitably, given the sums at stake, Bonnant appealed, taking the case to the Federal Supreme Court, the highest court in Switzerland. 'Mme Rybolovleva won the first round. She has partially lost the second round. There will be a third round,' he promised. In addition, the court of appeal awarded joint parental rights over their daughter Anna, while Elena had received sole rights initially.

On Dmitry's side, they rejoiced in the fact that the sum awarded to the opposing party approximately corresponded to the amount that the AS Monaco chairman had been ready to offer at the time his wife had filed for divorce, and he had accepted that she would not go back on her decision. In *La Tribune de Genève*, Bersheda justified the verdict, stating that Elena had been aware of the transfers to the trusts while they were still married:

> You have to imagine what it was like at the time. In Russia, all the big business leaders were afraid of 'corporate raids'. The ten richest men, women and families all created trusts, often in Cyprus, to protect their fortune. For my client, it was also a way of managing his succession in favour of his daughters … The civil code relating to this is exceedingly simple. All existing assets at the time of the divorce are to be divided in two. In fact, this case reflects the divorce of two people married with acquisitions, but who became billionaires.

There have been other spectacular developments, such as when Elena was arrested on the tarmac of a Cyprus airport after disembarking from a private flight in February 2014 and then interrogated by Limassol police. Trustees of one of Rybolovlev's Cypriot trusts lodged a complaint against Elena, accusing her of having stolen a unique diamond, which was estimated at €25 million.

The precious stone had been purchased in March 2008 at Graff Diamonds in London, and was an asset of one of the trusts set up in favour of their daughters. And while Elena had been authorised to wear the diamond, her application for a divorce nine months later had changed the situation. She had been officially requested, by way of three letters, to return it. The letters remained unanswered, leading to the

complaint. Examined at length, she provided the requested documents and was released with no charges being laid
against her.

'The particularities of Cypriot law will not defeat me, and
the legal protection that Mr Rybolovlev seems to enjoy on
the island will not be sufficient to impede the law,' seethed
Bonnant, alluding to the influence he suggests Rybolovlev
has benefited from since acquiring an almost 10 per cent
share in the Bank of Cyprus in 2010.[102] This was via Odella
Resources, a trust in his name and that of his two daughters.

This legal and fiscal battle against a backdrop of the va-
lidity of offshore companies, and the public airing of their
dispute continued to intrigue tabloids. Some have called this
war of attrition the 'most expensive divorce in history', ahead
of those of Rupert Murdoch and Silvio Berlusconi, even
though following the second judgment this is no longer the
case. Investigator and author Pierre Lorrain, an expert on the
USSR and Russia, has looked on during the settling of scores:

> Like Roman Abramovich, Dmitry Rybolovlev doesn't enjoy
> being in the limelight, while usually Russians like being
> talked about. Due to its special nature, his divorce was a
> media soap opera that attracted attention. Over there, in
> this type of case, the population (even women) usually takes
> the man's side. Lots of people thought, 'She's asking for four

---

102 A state establishment where deposits over €100,000 lost 47.5 per cent of their value,
     as part of a rescue package bail out granted to the island in the spring of 2013.

billion and she still lives in Switzerland, that's a bit much, isn't it?' Let's just say that the Russians sympathise.[103]

Elena Rybolovleva, co-owner of the house at Cologny, still lives on the edge of Lake Geneva. Her ex-husband only returns in exceptional circumstances, having left the country in 2011 for Monaco without any regrets. Seven years after the outbreak of hostilities and the painful divorce, the drama still wasn't over. But it could have been resolved once and for all in June 2012. An agreement had been reached for nearly 700 million Swiss francs in favour of Elena, before the deal was aborted at the last minute. She had demanded a single, one-off cash payment. He had refused. Other propositions were drawn up, again to no effect. But finally on 20 October 2015, taking everyone by surprise, the two parties reached a compromise, formalising their divorce amicably. They wrote an eight-line joint statement in three languages (French, English, and Russian).

It stated that 'both parties have agreed to terminate all legal proceedings in the divorce case and the ancillary proceedings in any jurisdiction', promising to 'definitively withdraw any claims against each other and against any person and entity connected with them'. It was a way of ending what had been 'a difficult time for them and their family'.

This final scene was sudden and unexpected. The amount

---

103   Interview with the author.

agreed on was not specified, although the sum must have been close to the amount that the court of justice ruled that Rybolovlev should pay in the second instance, approximately €500 million for Elena Rybolovleva.

With amounts such as these at stake, confidentiality is a given. The saga of the 'most expensive divorce in history' had an unexpected epilogue and would be due for a name change – what a shame for the lawyers. The third round that Bonnant had hoped for, before the Federal Supreme Court, which is the highest court in Switzerland, was not to be.

The timing of the end of this bitter negotiation, relieving the Rybolovlevs of never-ending legal proceedings, was no accident. A few days after having married Juan Sartori, an international businessman from Uruguay, at the Geneva town hall in the presence of both parents, Ekaterina held her religious wedding on Skorpios. The island, which she owns, was the location for this moment of good fortune on 21 October 2015, the day after the disclosure of the statement concerning the amicable agreement for the divorce. It was to be another wedding on this small piece of paradise, exactly forty-seven years (give or take a day) after the marriage between Jackie Bouvier Kennedy and Aristotle Onassis on a rainy afternoon in 1968.

Rybolovlev's son-in-law, aged thirty-six, has a profile that is sure to please: born in Montevideo before heading to Paris and Switzerland, he graduated from HEC Lausanne (the Faculty of Business and Economics of the University of Lausanne), before completing a year at Harvard studying economics and international finance. Sartori founded the Union Group in 2006, of which he is the president. The organisation owns interests in the sectors of agriculture, renewable energy, oil, and real estate, primarily in Latin America. And as Ekaterina shares a similar personality to her father, she decided on a quiet celebration, at the same place she had met her future husband, on the occasion of her twenty-fifth birthday party. 'We were determined to have a modest ceremony, solely in the presence of our family and close friends,' she said. 'The event was connected with Skorpios, just as all the important moments in my life have been.'

CHAPTER 13

PARADISE ISLAND

'There, there's only order, beauty: abundant, calm, voluptuous.' Published in his famous collection *Les Fleurs du Mal* (*The Flowers of Evil*), the refrain of Charles Baudelaire's poem 'Invitation to a Voyage' is a fitting one. The imposing white yacht with its minimalist lines bathes in the calm waters off the private island of Skorpios – baptised thus owing to its scorpion shape when seen from the sky. The anchor is dropped overboard. As the gangplank is thrown down, the cicadas sing amid the lush vegetation of this timeless setting, with its age-old olive trees, lemon trees, and paths lined with eucalyptus and cypress.

Skorpios, a piece of land located in western Greece, in the blue of the Ionian Sea, is Dmitry Rybolovlev's favourite haven. It is here that this fan of surfing, jet skis, and wakeboarding, generally accompanied by his partner, his parents, and his two daughters, enjoys lazing around and recharging his batteries; the place where he unwinds completely. When he's not out and about on his island, where he likes to walk, fish, swim, play tennis, or play an early evening four-a-side football match with his sports coach, the boat's crew, and friends, he remains quietly on his yacht. It's a slender, 67-metre-long craft, with a steel hull and the rest constructed of aluminium. Built in 2007 in the Netherlands, registered in the Cayman Islands, he named it *My Anna*, after his youngest daughter. With a cruising speed of 14,000 knots, or around 26 kilometres per hour, it can accommodate twelve guests and nineteen crew members. Its value is estimated at €70 million.

Until mid-April 2013, Skorpios was owned by horsewoman Athina Onassis-Roussel. But she had never been thrilled by this heavy 'inheritance' and its costly upkeep. In that respect, the 28-year-old Athina differs from her grandfather, Aristotle Onassis, who bought the island in 1962 and married Jacqueline Kennedy there six years later. Athina did not speak Greek and had already parted company with various family properties in the country; although baptised there, she had not made a public appearance in Skorpios for nine years. Ekaterina Dmitrievna Rybolovleva, also a competitive equestrian, had already crossed paths with the last living descendant of the Onassis family at show jumping contests.

Ekaterina had intimated to Athina that, should she ever decide to sell, she would be interested. So that's how it went, via the lawyers. According to a press release, 'a company acting in the interests of Ekaterina Rybolovleva has finalised the acquisition of a group of companies heretofore owned by Athina Onassis.' The press release specified that this was a 'long-term financial investment', which aimed to develop the infrastructure of Skorpios 'with the aid of environmentally-friendly technology'. The neighbouring island of Sparti was also part of the package.

The overall amount of the transaction came to €100 million. In section nine of his will, Aristotle Onassis had forbidden the sale of Skorpios, demanding that, if his descendants were unable to keep up with its maintenance costs, 'of around $100,000 per year', it should be gifted to the Greek state, to become a presidential residency or a resort. After a question posed by a conservative MP, the government accelerated an investigation into the sale conditions to verify whether they complied with the prerogatives and wishes of Aristotle Onassis. But the results of the investigation were not made public. And they did nothing to hamper the sale.

It was on Skorpios that, on 30 June 2015, a relaxed Dmitry Rybolovlev consented to tell me his story. Three hours of private non-stop discussion, detailing the various aspects of his life led him to forget his English class; the private tutor with blonde hair, not daring to disturb him, hung back in the doorway. Our appointment took place in the office of his yacht which is soberly decorated: an icon, videocassettes, DVDs, books, and little water bottles. Travelling in a rubber dinghy from the seaside resort of Lefkada, it takes ten minutes to reach the yacht which anchors off the opposite shore. Legend has it this was where Aphrodite, the goddess of beauty, was born. Along with Corfu, Paxos, Zakynthos, Ithaca, and Cephalonia, Lefkada forms the archipelago of the Ionian Islands.

It takes a good five hours by car from Athens to reach this end of the shoreline on the west coast. The trip is faster from the airports of Preveza or Ioannina, which have few tourists. Rybolovlev, when he is planning to stay at Skorpios, climbs into his private plane at Nice and flies to Preveza in two hours, followed by a short seven-minute helicopter trip to the yacht. As soon as he sets foot on this little island, he's a new man.

'I often went to Greece on holiday with my daughters and my parents when we first discovered Skorpios around ten years ago on a boat ride,' recalls Rybolovlev.

We immediately felt good there. I can even say that we fell in love with it. Some special vibrations govern this place. The connection with nature is total. Having family, friends and various other guests to stay here is a pleasure. Over the summer, we come here very often. This is our third summer here. We are modernising Skorpios bit by bit, taking care to do so in harmony with its environment, biodiversity and the history of the domain. Radical transformation is out of the question.[104]

---

104 Interview with the author.

In an interview with *Paris Match*, John, the former captain of the Onassis boat, who has become the soul and guardian of the site since it was sold by Athina, refines the statement:

> When Dmitry Rybolovlev and his daughter arrived, I thought they were brother and sister, given how youthful her father looked. We spent the evening together drinking and eating. So I picked up my guitar and hummed Greek and Russian tunes. I immediately saw that they were under its charm, bewitched by the island. After living here for eighteen years, maintaining this dreamland on my own, I am happy to see people who are going to invest and bring this sleeping beauty back to life.

If Rybolovlev feels so comfortable in Greece, it's also because connections with Russia abound, from the Cyrillic alphabet inspired by that of Greek to a mutual defiance towards the United States, as well as cultural and touristic affinities.

But the main thing the two countries have in common relates to the Orthodox religion. It is significant that one of Rybolovlev's first actions was to have the island blessed – he did the same for his Monegasque penthouse, calling in an Orthodox priest from Nice. It is also no surprise that he has undertaken, on several occasions, a pilgrimage to Mount Athos, perched at an altitude of 2,030 metres. This is a site that seems to exist outside of time, where daily entry is limited to 100 Orthodox and ten non-Orthodox visitors.

'It is a truly unique place,' Rybolovlev says of this holy mountain located in Macedonia in the north of Greece. Its reputation comes from the twenty Orthodox monasteries that have been established on its flanks and the surrounding area for more than ten centuries. The monks of this Halkidiki peninsula, while they are connected to the Hellenic Republic, live there in an autonomous community and, to keep temptation at bay, women are still forbidden there.

In Rybolovlev's mind, Mount Athos is associated with the Conception Convent, also called the Zachatyevsky monastery. This place of worship buzzes in the heart of Moscow. Built in 1360 and closed by the Bolsheviks in 1918, it only opened again in the early 1990s. Its latest renovation was funded by the billionaire and mainly concerned the Cathedral of the Nativity of Theotokos. This donation of €17.5 million in 2010, which enabled its re-creation, earned him the honour of first ranked in the order of Saint Seraphim of Sarov awarded by Patriarch Kirill or Cyril I, the highest dignitary of the Russian Orthodox Church, with over 100 million followers. The Patriarch Kirill would also look favourably on Rybolovlev's funding of the Saint-Nicolas Cathedral in Cyprus in the second-largest city on the island, in Limassol, on the Mediterranean coast. This Russian church received the *imprimatur* from the Archbishop Chrysostomos II, the highest Cypriot Orthodox authority.

On Skorpios, Rybolovlev is following in the wake of Aristotle Socrates Onassis. One of the most illustrious of Greeks, among the wealthiest men on earth and part of the international jet set, Onassis was born in Smyrna (now Izmir) in 1906 in what was not yet Turkey but the Ottoman Empire. He died sixty-nine years later, in March 1975. But Skorpios is not Rybolovlev's only connection with Onassis. The Greek shipping magnate also profoundly marked the Monegasque landscape.

Onassis moved there in 1952, three years after Prince Rainier III's ascension to the throne, when the young monarch of twenty-five succeeded his grandfather Louis II of Monaco. Onassis took over the Société des Bains de Mer de Monaco, the control tower of the principality's economy, from real estate to banking, hospitality, and tourism. Although their fates were never intertwined, Onassis and Rybolovlev's paths go in similar directions and are the stuff of legend – the epic tale of the man who chose to be buried on Skorpios, his island of predilection, is by no means banal.

The son of a rich tobacco trader, Aristotle Socrates Onassis was six years old when his mother, Penelope, died of kidney failure. Onassis would be raised by his grandmother. In 1922, Smyrna was sacked by the army of Mustafa Kemal and the Greeks chased out of Asia Minor by the Turks. Aristotle's father was sent to a prisoner-of-war camp, the family home was occupied by a Turkish general, and the women were sent away. Aristotle first sought refuge at his uncle's house in Athens and later emigrated to Argentina. In Buenos Aires, which had a large Greek community, he sold cigarettes made from tobacco balls that had been flown out from Athens. Carlos Gardel, one of the most famous singers in the history of tango, was mad about them. Onassis opened a tobacco factory, which also proved successful. Aged twenty-five, he had already made his first million dollars.

Intuitively, he bought six cargo ships from the Canadian government. Once again, fortune smiled on him. He had the ships registered in Panama to reduce tolls and taxes, taking advantage of flags of convenience. In 1938, he moved into oil tankers, large ones, one of the first business tycoons to do so; Onassis owned more than 100 super tankers at the time of his death.

In the early 1950s Onassis opened the offices of Olympic Maritime, the holding that supervised his oil company, above the port of Monte Carlo. Waters lapped at the sides of the *Christina O*, the former Canadian battleship that had participated in the 1944 D-Day landings of the Allied forces in Normandy, and which had since been transformed by the power of the American dollar into a gleaming 99-metre-long yacht. Ava Gardner, Marlene Dietrich, Marilyn Monroe, King Farouk of Egypt, John Wayne, the Aga Khan, and Sir Winston Churchill all travelled aboard this vessel on ultra-chic leisure cruises.

Alongside the playboy lifestyle the business continued. Via dozens of Panamanian businesses Onassis became the primary shareholder of the Société des Bains de Mer (SBM). The creation of the SBM by order of Prince Charles III in 1863 was a seminal act. This organisation transformed a village of 1,150 people along the coast of Les Spélugues (the 'small caves'), who were mainly living off the exportation of lemon and olive oil, into a glamorous rock. The SBM was first supported by businessman François Blanc, who built up a solid reputation by transforming the German thermal city of Homburg[105] into Europe's gambling capital, with the construction of a casino there in 1842.

Hoping to draw inspiration from the success of the Germanic cities that were prospering from slot machines, and aware that France and Italy did not authorise gambling, Prince Charles III recruited Blanc, who invested his own money into developing the SBM and extending its influence. Soon the Monte Carlo casino, the Café de Paris and the Hôtel de Paris emerged. Onassis was to be one of their worthy successors. The Greek installed his offices in the former villa of Marie Blanc, François Blanc's rich widow, who had the Opéra de Monte Carlo built by prominent architect Charles Garnier.

Prince Rainier III, aware that it would be a good idea to invest in tourism and international congresses to pursue the development of the principality, was the first to commend Onassis's ambitions. This was the same Rainier who, on 18–19 April 1956, in a civil ceremony followed by a religious one, married 27-year-old American actress Grace Kelly, a Hitchcock heroine (*Dial M for Murder*, *Rear Window*, *To Catch a Thief*), who had won an Oscar the previous year for *The Country Girl*.

---

105 This town, located in the state of Hesse, now goes by the name of Bad Homburg vor der Höhe.

During the event – at which nearly all of Hollywood was in attendance, as well as François Mitterrand, then France's Minister of Justice and in this capacity the representative of the socialist government of Guy Mollet – the hydroplane of Onassis rained down red and white carnations, the national flower and the colour of the Monegasque flag. The munificent reception was held aboard the *Christina O*. The paparazzi were on the case and the 'wedding of the century' – 30 million television viewers watched its broadcast – made the couple one of the most closely observed in the world.

Rainier, who was to rule for fifty-six years, was nicknamed the 'founding prince'. A powerful ruler, he ordered the construction of the new neighbourhood of Fontvieille, built on the sea by reclaiming 220,000m^2 of land, along with a new port, thus threatening a diplomatic war with General de Gaulle based on a tax dispute. This crisis would incite France to temporarily blockade Monaco and resulted in the signing of numerous agreements, since the principality had become an institutional monarchy in December 1962. Suffice to say that Rainier did not like sharing power. And Onassis had become, in this respect, a thorn in his side.

In 1966, the SBM, despite being the country's main business while only contributing four per cent of its revenue to the nation's budget, underwent a radical shift: it became a company under private law, of which the state was the majority shareholder. The message was clear. Begrudgingly, under threat of a nationalisation of gambling, Onassis had to concede the SBM to Rainier. Nine years after having been its main shareholder, the man with the big black spectacles was thus expediently ousted from the principality. Bidding farewell to the Rock, Onassis headed for Skorpios, which had become his home port, one he departed from regularly to conduct business and travel the world.

The hand of fate did not spare the shipping magnate. He never recovered from the death of his son Alexander at the age of twenty-four. Alexander had been the boss of Onassis's airline company, Olympic Airways. In 1973, during a training flight above Athens, Alexander's seaplane crashed into the sea. Like his father Aristotle, his aunt Artemis, and his sister Christina, who died aged thirty-seven of a pulmonary oedema in her bathtub in Argentina, Alexander was buried on Skorpios, under a white marble slab near the chapel.

Monaco, a yacht bearing his daughter's name, his clear talent for business, and Skorpios: all of this makes for many points of intersection between Onassis and Rybolovlev. Is it deliberate? The Russian, who favours discretion while the Greek opted for ostentatious displays, dismisses the theory with a wave of his hand: 'Skorpios is certainly a place charged with history, a history that I'm well aware of, just as I'm well aware of Onassis's story. But I have no desire to follow in his footsteps. Yet, it is true that, in Monaco, I live in a place that he once frequented, even if, in the meantime, the building was destroyed and then rebuilt.'

While he led the transformation of Monaco into a capital

of socialites, Aristotle Onassis influenced the fate of Skorpios to an even greater extent. Initially, he wanted to settle 15 kilometres away, on the neighbouring island of Ithaca, Ulysses's former kingdom. He eventually favoured Skorpios only because he was unable to convince the thousands of inhabitants of Ithaca to live elsewhere.

He did not regret it. Onassis acquired the island in 1962 for 3.5 million drachma, the equivalent of about £10,000. This was logical: the place was deserted. The landscape was idyllic, but there was nothing there, except for a small house, a stone chapel, and the ruins of an olive press, all of which dated from the late nineteenth century. Onassis was to transform the island through his great wealth, shipping in tonnes of fine sand from Salamis Island to create new beaches including 'Jackie Beach', planting hundreds of trees of various species, transporting fresh water from a neighbouring island, excavating a port for his yacht, and building a road several kilometres long. The work took five years. Trees, flowers, private beaches, guesthouses, and a farm to raise animals and cultivate fruit and vegetables: the landscape was gradually aligned with his dreams of grandeur.

To pay tribute to the residents of Lefkada as well as to encourage their acceptance of him, Onassis prompted the diva Maria Callas, with whom he had a tumultuous relationship, to give a concert in Lefkada. Moved by her generosity and voice, the village barber gave Callas a canary, which she became totally enamoured with.

But it was Jacqueline Kennedy who changed the international status of Skorpios. Onassis invited President Kennedy's widow, twenty years younger than himself, aboard his yacht and took great delight in seducing her, all the more so as, a few years previously, he had clashed with the Kennedy clan, who threatened to have him imprisoned unless he stopped negotiating with the king of Saudi Arabia to obtain a monopoly on the transport of Saudi oil. Onassis had attended the funeral in Washington of the President, assassinated at forty-six years of age on 22 November 1963 in Dallas. Five years later, he married JFK's widow in the Orthodox chapel of his island. Only twenty-five guests were invited to the wedding on Sunday 20 October 1968. The area was under close surveillance by an impressive security team while, out at sea, hundreds of reporters and photographers lay in wait.

This is not so much the case now that Rybolovlev's eldest daughter is the owner, even if Ekaterina has held several parties, including one to mark her twenty-fifth birthday, in the spring of 2014, with around 100 guests, including a number of prestigious VIPs. Paparazzi are unwelcome and tourist boats no longer venture near the shores of Skorpios now that it has resumed a semblance of activity – because Dmitry Rybolovlev does intend to restore its former glory.

With this in mind, he has elected a relative to oversee operations on the island: Andrey Konogorov, his cousin, the son of his mother's sister. A professional engineer, two years his senior, Konogorov worked alongside Rybolovlev at Uralkali, where he moved up the ranks to the position of board member. Rybolovlev has handed Kongorov the keys to the 200-hectare domain, and it is up to him to supervise the smooth functioning of Skorpios, which employs more than thirty people on a day-to-day basis. Konogorov admits he is proud of his mission and explains how he became the head of operations:

After leaving Uralkali once it was sold, then directing a bank, I moved to London for several months with my wife, to study English. I then returned to service to focus on the restructuring of the Bank of Cyprus. In the summer of 2012, I was a free man. I took advantage of this period to hunt, fish, and travel. A year later, I was still enjoying life and having a nice time. I'd never experienced that before. The phone rang. Dmitry wanted to see what I'd been up to. Immediately, he set me a kind of challenge: 'Andrey, you speak English and you like fishing. So come to Skorpios.' I spent three days there in September with my wife. And I fell in love with the colours of that magnificent sea and that wild land. Dmitry asked if I would like to spend some time there. 'What would I have to do there?' I asked. 'It would be up to you to organise, plan, and modernise while respecting the landscape.'

Asked why he was chosen, Konogorov admits he doesn't know: 'Dmitry didn't tell me anything. No need. That's his choice. He often has powerful intuitions; they're inexplicable. Besides which, he knows and trusts me.'[106]

Konogorov doesn't live year-round on Skorpios and often returns to Perm. But, from early spring and for the whole of summer, he spends at least two weeks there each month. He has immersed himself in the place, devouring everything that concerns the legend of Onassis to honour his memory. For instance, the Pink House where Jacqueline Kennedy used to stay has been renovated (the whole floor was peeling) and a bedroom in the form of a museum has been installed. Konogorov also takes care to develop the island's resources, using local products for meals, frequenting the supermarkets of the region, and buying his diesel for the boats locally rather than in Patras, as was once the case. He has also launched a vast agricultural programme, so now Skorpios produces its own potatoes, tomatoes, onions, and watermelons.

Since Rybolovlev is a wine enthusiast, Konogorov has set about planting grapes, enough to be able to make their own wine five years from now. Among the projects underway: rainwater catchments; the installation of solar panels; the replacement of age-old electric cables and water pipes; the purchase of electric cars for getting about; and the construction of a new farm with the help of a Greek company. The island is entirely equipped with Wi-Fi and a fire-fighting system. Last, but certainly not least, stables are being constructed so

---

106 Interview with the author.

that Ekaterina, the official owner of the island, can indulge her passion of horse riding.

> I love this job. Although I love fishing, I am so busy that I don't have the time to get out my rod. It's almost as though I've become a farmer! I manage the project, but the work is done as a team and the system works even when I'm not here. There are more and more personnel. Skorpios never stops growing,

says Konogorov enthusiastically.

'We also have sheep, goats, and chickens. In the long run, we will produce our own cheese and yoghurt. Katia and Dmitry love Greek yoghurt. We want to be increasingly autonomous and self-sufficient. Skorpios is a Garden of Eden. Basically, it's paradise.'

According to Korina Fasouli, a lawyer based near Athens who has acted in connection with the Rybolovlev family, the development of Skorpios has been undertaken in an environmentally friendly way. 'It's a boon for the region. The legend of Onassis lives on through Rybolovlev,' says the associate member of the law firm CFG&A. 'It's important because for us Greeks, and for the rest of the world for that matter, Skorpios is a symbol. This region of Lefkada, for geological reasons, is littered with small islands, with a special ecosystem and microclimate, which allows for varied agriculture.'[107]

---

107 Interview with the author.

With the purchase of Skorpios in April 2013 and the fact that now, for day-to-day operations, there are over thirty employees from the surrounding towns labouring there, the region is satisfied. All the more so in that Dmitry Rybolovlev is a generous patron. In June 2015, in a country stricken by the austerity crisis and threatened with being kicked out of Europe, while Aléxis Tsípras, the Greek Prime Minister and leader of the far-left coalition, led the charge, Rybolovlev gave (through the intermediary of the charity organisation created with his daughter) €20,000 to the Lefkada hospital, to cover doctors' wages. He also bought vehicles for the town to encourage school transport, particularly of disabled children.

Ioannis Kartanos, deputy mayor of Lefkada when Rybolovlev bought Skorpios, was completely won over. Also the chairman of the association of the hotels in the region, which has 140 of them, including his own, this former manager of the football club of Panathinaikos in Athens talks about his first encounter with the Russian:

Like many others, I was able to see the improvements of the Onassis era, which made Skorpios famous and created a lot of employment. When they arrived, Dmitry Rybolovlev and his daughter Katia invited us over, the mayor of the city Kostas Aravanis and I, in order to present their project to us. They were very friendly, kind, and open to suggestions. We felt at ease and felt as though we had known each other for a long time. From the outset, he asked us: 'What can I do for the island?' He insisted on involving the local residents. Local retailers were called upon. This was primordial, because, in recent years, Skorpios had been inactive or virtually inactive. It revived interest and curiosity in the island.[108]

Kartanos mentions that the former holding midfielder of AS Monaco, Andréas Zíkos, the first Greek player to be a finalist in the Champions League in 2004, was also invited to dinner on the island. 'Dmitry Rybolovlev was wearing clothes from the island. His parents were there, as were the local councillors. The atmosphere was relaxed. And we drank good local wine. Even if he doesn't seek publicity, he is a kind of messiah for Skorpios.'

During the first exchanges, Kartanos whispered to Rybolovlev's daughter that a statue in Onassis's likeness existed in the port of Lefkada. 'I added that, perhaps, in a few years' time, there would also be a statue of Rybolovlev near it. Dmitry listened and smiled.'

---

108 Interview with the author.

CHAPTER 14

PICASSO, FREE PORTS, FRAUD: THE MASTERPIECES OF DISCORD

A two-part dramatised documentary *The Divine Eye* cel-
ebrates the centenary of the Pushkin State Museum of
Fine Arts. This state establishment, in the heart of Moscow,
prides itself on its collection of 670,000 works, from Ancient
Greece, Rome, and Egypt to Botticelli, Rembrandt, and Picasso. Leonid Parfenov, a renowned Russian television journalist,
is the producer and presenter of *The Divine Eye*. His patron
and producer is none other than Dmitry Rybolovlev, who,
on the DVD cover, explains that he and the director 'the idea
that Russians feel European through beauty. I am convinced
that Russia and Europe are two cultures that are totally
complementary.'

An art lover with a preference for the first half of the twentieth century (contemporary works don't particularly move
him), Rybolovlev has satisfied his curiosity by visiting ex-
hibitions in the most famous institutions across the globe.

'Before finding out if it is a masterpiece or not, I first look for the emotion in a work. I like the impressionists and post-impressionism, particularly Modigliani and Picasso,'[109] he says, adding that the Musée d'Orsay in Paris and the Metropolitan in New York have earned his special approval.

But in addition to being a passion, art can also be a profitable investment. Paintings, etchings, statues, stamps, or antique objects are not calculated as part of any tax on wealth. 'Products' such as these (which can be sold for a profit) are exempt, thus enabling tax optimisation. Just like wine and jewellery, art is a flourishing market, with objects holding their investment value. Rybolovlev began collecting works with his ex-wife with a view to decorating their family home in Cologny as the former owner had removed his art, but left behind a state-of-the-art lighting system. The spaces had to be filled in.

The couple's planned replica of the Palace of Versailles' Petit Trianon never saw the light of day, but the art masterpieces did. Given their values, and to avoid paying substantial insurance, they were first stored in the Geneva free ports, 150,000m² of warehouses, half of which are under the surveillance of customs officials. Owned mostly by the canton of Geneva, the high-security area provides a huge duty-free zone, where merchandise is not subject to custom duties or import VAT. Seven hundred people work on the site and around thirty deposits and withdrawals of objects take place

109   Interview with the author.

daily. The goods stored there have an estimated total value of €80 billion.

Over the years the Rybolovlev family trusts (the legal owners of the works, which will represent an asset for Rybolovlev's descendants) have acquired around forty masterpieces. As he is not an expert or a historian, he relied on Swiss national Yves Bouvier, head of Natural Le Coultre since 1997, and a specialist in the transport and storage of works of art, to build up this prestigious collection.

Bouvier's father was the owner of the venerable family business founded in 1859, but in his hands the company focused on moving services. His son transformed it, in the process becoming the primary tenant at the Geneva free ports, where Yves Bouvier rents half the total space. He has also developed subsidiaries in Singapore and Luxembourg. The 53-year-old businessman was introduced to the Rybolovlevs around fifteen years ago by a friend of the couple, a Swiss national of Bulgarian origin, Tania Rappo. At the time, her husband was Elena Rybolovleva's dentist.

Rappo speaks Russian, has excellent interpersonal skills, and soon became a close friend of the couple. In fact, the relationship became so close that she was chosen to be the godmother of Anna, their youngest daughter who was born in 2001. Rappo told *Monaco-Matin* that:

> Elena is like a small, fragile bird. I helped her with her letters
> and papers … And then we lost touch with one another as I

travelled frequently at the time. Sometime later, we got back in touch, and she introduced her husband to me. He is a fascinating man, but who immediately makes your blood run cold. He is extremely harsh, distant, and doesn't speak much. The day after we first met, he called me saying he wanted me to help him become a member of the Geneva Golf Club. I also helped them with a passport problem ... I was not paid for that, and I would never have asked.'

Rappo is the key to understanding the whole astonishing story. When Rybolovlev started to think about building up an art collection, he turned to her. She was the one who enabled him to acquire his first work of art, *The Circus* by Marc Chagall.

That's how I really discovered the art business, through various intermediaries, the painting, which was worth €5 million initially, was going to be sold to him for €8 million. Via my contacts, I found out who the sellers were. I introduced these people directly to Rybolovlev, thereby saving him €3 million. And that was the one and only time there was a direct financial relationship between the two of us. Moreover, he paid me €50,000. But it is also important to note that, sometime later, he sold it on for €12 million!

It was via Rappo that Rybolovlev came to know Bouvier. The understanding between the two men was immediate. Their interests converged – the Russian billionaire had the money, while the Swiss entrepreneur possessed the network and the expertise. Everything operated with the utmost discretion. Via the intermediary of this art world professional, Rybolovlev invested just under €2 billion in thirty-seven master artworks. His collection included works by Van Gogh, Klimt, El Greco, Rothko, Modigliani, Gauguin, Renoir, Rodin, Matisse, Picasso, Monet, Magritte, Toulouse-Lautrec, Degas, da Vinci, and Giacometti. Among the collection were some truly monumental works, notably *Salvator Mundi* (*Saviour of the World*), an oil painting on wood depicting Christ making the sign of the benediction, restored and authenticated in 2009 as being by Leonardo da Vinci; and *Les Noces de Pierrette* (*The Marriage of Pierrette*), painted in 1905 by Pablo Picasso in his blue period at the Bateau-Lavoir in Montmartre. Everything seemed idyllic. But this was an illusion that was soon shattered.

On 9 January 2015, Accent Delight International and Xitrans Finance[110] lodged a criminal complaint with Monaco's public

110   In April 2016, 'the Panama Papers', the leaking of 11.5 million files belonging to Panama legal firm Mossack Fonseca, were published, revealing the hidden face of offshore finance and tax havens. Among others, Xitrans Finance Limited was mentioned. *Le Monde*, one of the many media outlets that analysed the documents, suggested works of art would have been purchased under its name, thereby concealing them and putting them out of reach of Rybolovlev's ex-wife at the time of their divorce. For Tetiana Bersheda, it was a question of 'succession planning and protection of assets'. In *Nice-Matin*, the Russian's lawyer clarified: 'The article fails to state that the Rybolovlev ex-spouses announced via a joint statement on 20 October 2015, that they had concluded an amicable divorce, that they had terminated all outstanding legal proceedings, and that Mrs Rybolovlev had definitively withdrawn all claims towards Mr Rybolovlev and any person or entity connected with him.' She added that her client 'had never used offshore companies to conceal his assets. The creation of Xitrans Finance dates from 2002, or six years prior to the beginning of divorce proceedings, and so has nothing to do with the divorce of the Rybolovlev spouses.'

prosecutor. The two companies, based in the British Virgin Islands and owned by Cypriot trusts whose beneficiaries are Rybolovlev's daughters and Rybolovlev himself, levelled serious allegations against Bouvier. They claimed they had been over-billed to the tune of almost $1 billion. The Rybolovlev clan were convinced that Bouvier, mandated by them as an intermediary between 2003 and 2014 (negotiating prices for a commission of two per cent per transaction) took advantage of this status to increase the value of each work. He thus pocketed, in addition to the commission, large margins that the Rybolovlevs maintain they knew nothing about.

The following month, on 25 February, a tremor shook the art market: Bouvier, who was not aware that the complaint existed, was arrested on the Rock. He had arrived that morning by private jet from Geneva via Nice, to meet with Rybolovlev. Instead he was met by around ten police officers, who handcuffed him.

That evening in the company of Prince Albert, the chairman of AS Monaco watched from the box at the Emirates Stadium as his team triumphed against Arsenal in the final game before the quarter-finals of the Champions League. Bouvier did not watch the match – he was being interrogated by police. And he had no idea what was happening to him. He explains that he had travelled to the Rock because Rybolovlev 'wasn't able to pay the final instalment of the last painting bought from my company, the most beautiful Rothko in the world, *No. 6 (Violet, Green, and Red)*.'

Bouvier, who up until that moment had enjoyed a spotless

reputation, spent seventy-two hours in custody. He was charged with 'fraud' and as an 'accomplice in money laundering' against Dmitry Rybolovlev, and was placed under court supervision, with a €10 million bail. In addition, Tania Rappo was charged with 'money laundering'. After ninety-six hours in police custody, she was placed under court supervision with no bail. However, her company accounts at various Monegasque banking institutions were blocked. She was suspected of having received secret commissions paid by Bouvier on each purchase. On 12 March 2015, the difficult series of events continued for Bouvier: his assets in Singapore, where he is domiciled, and in Hong Kong were frozen.

And so for the public, the 'Bouvier Affair' began, an inextricable maze of a story that is only just beginning and most likely will carry on for years. It is a story about art, passion, friendship, lies, and betrayal. It is a saga worthy of a detective novel, deserving of several volumes. It is a story where all concerned get burnt.

A Swiss journalist who has been following this gripping saga and who prefers to remain anonymous says:

Bouvier is a prominent citizen who considered himself as powerful as the Swiss minister for the economy. In 2014, he joined the ranks of the 200 largest fortunes in the country. With the success of his free port in Singapore, in a high-security building at the end of the airport tarmac, and with a new project in Beijing, he was on the rise, his savoir-faire recognised throughout the world. Everything was stopped in its tracks by the complaint that Rybolovlev lodged. Rybolovlev is now trying to crush him, and he just won't give up – it's not his style. He went to the best school of business there is – making your fortune in Russia in the 1990s. He is playing the legal card to its fullest extent. What surprises me, though, is the total trust he had in Bouvier, from the beginning. It's almost an eastern trust, bordering on naivety. We're talking about €2 billion here, invested in paintings.[111]

'The key figure in all this is Tania Rappo, a close friend of the family who we got to know in Geneva. She's the one that introduced me to Bouvier. I trusted her, and she took advantage of our friendship. Without Rappo, there would be no Bouvier,' explains Rybolovlev, simply.

An elegant woman in her sixties, Tania Rappo describes with great dismay how eight police officers arrived at her home with a search warrant. She doesn't hesitate to attack Rybolovlev directly as the cause of her ordeal.

'To understand what kind of person Mr Rybolovlev is,' she says,

I have to clarify that saw him about four or five times a year, in these past years. The second-to-last time I saw him, it was

111   Interview with the author.

for his birthday last November, with lots of other people. The day before I was arrested, on 24 February, Rybolovlev had invited my husband and me to his home, for dinner with his father and mother. He kissed me, he encouraged me to drink. He even said, 'Have another vodka!' When I replay those events in my head, it is very clear that he knew I was going to be arrested.

Rybolovlev has stuck to his guns. The stakes are huge. He is convinced he is in the right and wonders how his former representative will pay him back. However, the Swiss art transporter was also getting ready for the fray. And so, on 22 July 2015, Bouvier counter-attacked by filing a new suit in Monaco, calling for the proceedings to be nullified. On 24 August, Singapore unfroze his assets. Ten or so days later, in contrast to the High Court of Justice in Hong Kong, Hong Kong's Court of Appeal in turn ordered the unfreezing of his assets after the withdrawal of proceedings. It was a welcome relief.

But Rybolovlev was determined not to give in. His blind fury at Bouvier had begun on 31 December 2014. He was spending the New Year at St Barts in the Caribbean. While dining in the restaurant of a five-star hotel, surrounded by white, sandy beaches, Rybolovlev was introduced to Sandy Heller, a New York art consultant. Heller has the ear of Steve Cohen, a powerful hedge fund manager, whose fortune in 2011 was estimated at $8 billion. The American is also a registered collector, purchasing *The Dream* by Picasso in 2013 for $155 million. Heller and Rybolovlev discussed Modigliani's *Nu Couché au Coussin Bleu* (*Reclining Nude with Blue Cushion*). The Russian had bought it two years earlier for $118 million and discovered that the artwork had been sold by Cohen for $93 million just a few days before. Suffice to say that Rybolovlev spent a rather difficult end-of-year celebration.

That was to be the beginning of a downward spiral for Bouvier. The Geneva authorities, flanked by Monegasque police inspectors, searched Natural Le Coultre and the free ports. Bouvier had suffered a loss of prestige. Some people turned away from him (in this world, reserve and secrecy are crucial), and his initiatives lost momentum, such as the R4 art city project on Ile Seguin in Boulogne-Billancourt, an art centre for which he was the major shareholder and had committed to investing €150 million.

After his release, Bouvier could not contain his fury against Rybolovlev and denied any wrongdoing. The view of Rybolovlev's lawyer is quite different: 'It's not the price paid for the artworks that is the problem. My clients (the beneficiaries of the family trust) were fooled by the status of Yves Bouvier. Their trust was initially deliberately gained and then betrayed by fraudulent tactics', argues Bersheda.

For almost fifteen years, Yves Bouvier portrayed himself to them as their representative and advisor, charged with finding and negotiating artworks at the best price, on behalf of them, and to their advantage. But actually, he worked to his own advantage by pocketing the hidden profit on each transaction, thus creating a loss for my clients totalling almost $1 billion. And he did that via offshore companies and accounts.[112]

Each legal victory triggered additional rounds of invective. When Singapore unfroze the assets, judging that there was no risk of Bouvier dissipating his assets, he raised the stakes. Regarding Rybolovlev, he told *La Tribune de Genève* on 31 August 2015:

> What he has done to me is irreparable. I developed my business in a discreet manner, away from the spotlight, and now I find myself attacked on all fronts: criminal, civil, media, private, professional, and even the freeports. Mr Rybolovlev wants to send me to the gulag; he wants to 'kill' Bouvier. Well, then it's war; I won't lose to them – not him or his lawyer, who was also actively involved in these transactions. They have fooled the legal system and have destroyed my reputation. I will destroy the only thing that this Russian billionaire, hidden away in Monaco, holds dear: his fortune. By launching this assault, he has already 'burnt' his collection. If he wanted to sell it now, he wouldn't get half of its value.

---

112   Interview with the author.

Bouvier has made the quarrel a personal one. To see it through, he has surrounded himself with a battery of high-powered lawyers. Among them is Francis Szpiner from Paris, who has constantly denounced the conditions that led to his client's arrest on the Rock, lambasting a 'biased' order by Monaco Public Prosecutor Jean-Pierre Dreno, and commenting with irony on how the inquiry opened with 'a swiftness that demands respect, on the same day as the complaint had been received'. He talks of a 'trap laid by the plaintiff', sniffing out a plot hatched in Gstaad during a society gala organised by a Geneva jeweller, at which Rybolovlev mingled with Philippe Narmino, director of the principality's Department of Justice and president of the Council of State, and Gérard Cohen, chief executive at Monaco HSBC, the bank which, according to Szpiner, produced false documents before his client's detention.

Complete nonsense says Bersheda. 'Dmitry Rybolovlev and Yves Bouvier got together regularly in Monaco for work meetings, in accordance with Mr Bouvier's mandate. They took place at least five times a year,' she reiterates. 'At Gstaad, the reality was quite different to the myth our adversaries have propagated. They were all participating in the same soirée, with around 100 guests. Which private conversation between the three men would we be talking about? For the accused parties to insinuate that a plot was hatched against them on that occasion is absurd. In Monaco and elsewhere, these people cross each other's paths regularly on various occasions, particularly charitable events.'

Compared to Szpiner, Luc Brossollet, a fellow Parisian lawyer, is considerably more discreet, notwithstanding a role in Dominique de Villepin's aborted 2012 French presidential campaign. A son and grandson of lawyers, head of his own firm, and in partnership with Olivier d'Antin since 1992, he is involved in media law, intellectual property, criminal law, and civil and commercial liability. Both he and his client were invited to express themselves in these pages.

'Dear Sir, Yves Bouvier does not intend to participate in your investigation. Yours sincerely,' he wrote by email on 26 June 2015.

It is indeed difficult to communicate about an affair that is continually (r)evolving. Former French President Jacques Chirac (for whom Szpiner was a close advisor and defender) used to joke, 'les emmerdes, ça vole toujours en escadrille [shit always flies in formation]!' Proof of the veracity of that epigram came on 14 September 2015, when Bouvier was charged in Paris with handling stolen goods after a claim was filed by Catherine Hutin-Blay, the daughter of Jacqueline Roque, Pablo Picasso's second wife.

She suspected Bouvier of having stolen two *gouache* paintings – *Tête de Femme* and *Espagnole à l'Eventail* – sold after having been restored, and acting as a broker to Accent Delight International, a company connected to Rybolovlev. Bouvier was questioned for two hours by the examining magistrate, Isabelle Rich-Flament, who had summoned him several months earlier and had issued an international arrest

warrant and an Interpol red notice against him before plac-
ing him under probation. He was released upon payment of
€5 million, of a total bail of €27 million (to be paid before
the end of the summer), a sum which corresponded to the
amount paid by Rybolovlev for the purchase of the works
that Hutin-Blay thought had been stored in a warehouse in
a Paris suburb since 2008. She swears that she was not aware
that the two paintings, as well as a series of fifty-eight drawings, were sold in 2010 and 2013 to Rybolovlev.

In May 2015, art dealer Olivier Thomas, a close friend of
Bouvier's who in fact replaced him as chairman of the board
of directors of the free port in Luxembourg when his friend
was targeted by the justice system, was placed under investigation by the Brigade de Répression du Banditisme, a special
unit of the French Ministry of the Interior focusing on serious crimes including major art theft. He is the manager of
Art Transit International, specialising in the transport and
storage of exceptional works, who Hutin-Blay had entrusted
with the storage of the paintings.

In midsummer, given the scale of the proceedings, Bouvier hired a spokesperson, Swiss-Italian communications
consultant Marc Comina. After Bouvier was charged,
Comina informed the press that Bouvier had immediately
made contact with the judge's Parisian office. 'He presented all the necessary documentation showing that he had
purchased Picasso's works on paper from a trust presented
as belonging to Catherine Hutin-Blay and had later sold

them on to Dimitri Rybolovlev.' He continued, as a token of good faith: 'If he acquired artworks for which he knew the provenance and which filled all due diligence criteria, and if through no will of his own, it should transpire that he had been mistaken, Yves Bouvier will turn against those that fooled him and will repay the injured party.'

According to Comina, the two 'paintings were not sold in secret', but 'were invoiced by Yves Bouvier's company MEI Invest, to adorn the walls of Dmitry Rybolovlev's chalet in Gstaad, in full view of all his guests.' He confirmed that they were destined to be exhibited in public and to feature in a book devoted to his collection. This wasn't enough to move Picasso's stepdaughter, whose lawyer claimed on the website of French magazine *Le Point* that she never gave 'her consent nor received payment for these sales, which had taken place without her knowledge. She is not a beneficiary of any trust and does not know Mr Bouvier.'

In the wake of this, Rybolovlev let fire again with a statement noting the indictment of Bouvier for the handling of stolen goods and for being placed under court supervision, 'as well as the past existence of an international warrant for his arrest.'

If these allegations against Mr Bouvier are proven correct, they reinforce the seriousness of the fraudulent practices of which Accent Delight International and Xitrans Finance believe themselves victims and for which an investigation is currently underway with the Monegasque justice system for forgery and fraud. In this context, Mr Bouvier and Mrs Rappo were charged on 28 February with fraud and money laundering. Accent Delight International and Xitrans Finance started civil legal proceedings in Singapore seeking compensation for these fraudulent practices. They maintain their absolute determination to see these proceedings through to the end.

Rybolovlev subsequently remitted the two Picasso paintings to France's specialist police division, the Brigade de Répression du Banditisme, in the presence of some photographers, 'for the purposes of expert appraisal' and with the sole aim, he said, 'of eliciting manifestations of truth'.

In what could be seen as a counterblow in the public relations fight, the September 2015 edition of *Vanity Fair* carried a ten-page exclusive: 'Oligarch versus Art Dealer: Revelations on the Case that is Causing Tremors in Monaco and Switzerland.' Former political editor at *Le Monde*, Hervé Gattegno, now editor-in-chief for investigative reporting at *Vanity Fair*, had an exclusive interview with Bouvier. The meeting occurred in the back room of one of Bouvier's favourite local Italian restaurants.

'That's where he told me how he had helped the Monegasque oligarch for twelve years, and in the utmost secrecy, to build up one of the most fabulous art collections in history, and how, having done that, he gambled – and won – on the price of each artwork.'

An infographic lists the masterpieces (including six Picasso and seven Modigliani works) acquired through the intermediary of Bouvier. It was not the first time that the magazine had focused on Rybolovlev. In November 2013, *Vanity Fair* published a ten-page in-depth report entitled 'Dmitry and Elena Rybolovlev: How to Divorce a Billionaire'. The article ended with:

> After five years of merciless confrontation, the former lovers of Perm have grown so far apart that they seem to live on two different planets. Elena heads a foundation that grants funds to some of the most chic events in Geneva's cultural life – on 15 July 2013, she was present at the exceptional recital given at Bellerive, on the shores of Lake Morat, by 22-year-old Russian pianist Daniil Trifonov. At the same time, Dmitry was going from stadium to soirée, focusing on strengthening his team and enhancing his prestige. The last we heard, they were still married.

The editor-in-chief of *Vanity Fair* was Michel Denisot – who it may be recalled was associated briefly with Rybolovlev when Monaco were trying to establish an accord with the French Football Federation as to their tax status. That came to naught, and Denisot's subsequent invoice for €100,000 was ignored.

Denisot – who claimed he was unaware the article was coming out – said in an interview in October 2014 on the publication of his memoir covering fifty years of professional life that he met Rybolovlev 'via a mutual acquaintance'. That acquaintance, according to a number of sources, was Yves Bouvier. Denisot and Bouvier attended the same soirées at the Cannes Film Festival. The Swiss was to introduce Denisot to Rybolovlev as 'the man you need in the world of football.'

Throughout these difficult proceedings, Rybolovlev had entrusted his lawyer, Bersheda, with the responsibility of coordinating a team that also included Mrs Géraldine Gazo in Monaco and, in Paris, two stars of the bar: Éric Dupond-Moretti, known as 'the Acquitor', and Jean-Michel Darrois. Rybolovlev also benefited from the influence of the media and public relations agency, Majorelle PR & Events. It was created by Anne Hommel, the former guru of crisis communication at Euro RSCG, who has worked with clients ranging from Dominique Strauss-Kahn to the satirical magazine *Charlie Hebdo*.

The case has sailed on, lubricated by vitriol and lawyers' fees, and is still springing surprises. In November 2015, Bouvier's request for an annulment by the Chamber of the Court of Appeal of Monaco was rejected. Five days later Rybolovlev and Bersheda found themselves in custody. The Monaco police interrogated them for two hours in the context of an investigation opened following a complaint lodged by Tania Rappo, for invasion of privacy. They were not charged. Rappo had accused them of having recorded a conversation without her knowledge during a dinner at Rybolovlev's home, two days before her and Bouvier's arrest; she claims the pirated recording was given to the principality's police by Bersheda, violating provisions in the criminal code.

Lawyers for Bersheda and Rybolovlev responded: 'They have simply succeeded in revealing the puerile and derisive nature of this case, and their aim is simply to create a smoke-screen and conceal the real activities denounced by the injured parties. The investigation concerning money laundering and fraud is in the hands of the investigating judge of Monaco and is ongoing.'

On 23 February 2016, a year after fraud charges were filed against Bouvier, it was Bersheda's turn to be charged, for invasion of privacy, in Monaco, after Rappo's comments were recorded on her mobile phone and transmitted to the Monaco police.

'It is a smokescreen to deflect us from the real issue, the attitude of art shipper Yves Bouvier,' commented Gérard Baudoux, Bersheda's counsel.

In 2017, Singapore's High Court partly satisfied Bouvier's request to transfer the case to Switzerland. The Court of Appeal then agreed with the art dealer, stating that Switzerland was 'distinctly a more appropriate forum than Singapore for the determination of the parties' dispute, and halting further legal proceedings in Singapore until the Swiss authorities could determine their own jurisdiction over the case.

'The court has been clear – Singapore is not the appropriate forum for this case. Now the plaintiffs have to decide whether to start again and initiate legal action outside of Singapore,' Ron Soffer, lead counsel for Bouvier, said in an emailed statement reported by Bloomberg.

Sergey Chernitsyn, a representative for Rybolovlev's family office, responded: 'The decision contains no findings on the substance of the case and merely constitutes another procedural incident in this complex international litigation. It opens a new avenue for litigation in Switzerland.'

As the French pop band Les Ritas Mitsouko once sang: *Les histoires d'amour finissent mal en général* (Love stories generally don't end well).[113] Nor do stories of friendship betrayed.

---

113   Lyric from 'Les Histoires d'A', from *The No Comprendo* album (Virgin France: 1986).

CHAPTER 15

CHAMPIONS

While hope, as ever in football, sprang eternal, Monaco's supporters approached the 2016–17 season in sanguine mood. Striker Zlatan Ibrahimović had left Paris Saint-Germain for Manchester United, but PSG would surely win their fifth successive Ligue 1 title regardless. Even without the self-styled 'King of Paris', PSG had won the pre-season Trophée des Champions – akin to England's FA Community Shield – crushing Lyon 4–1. So absolute was their dominance in the Austrian city of Klagenfurt, where the game was improbably staged, that PSG were 4–0 up in less than an hour.

This meant that PSG had won the last ten trophies available in French football (Ligue 1, Coupe de France, Coupe de la Ligue, and Trophée des Champions). At €521 million their revenue dwarfed that of every club including Monaco (€77 million). Attendances at Parc des Princes were six times those at Louis II, while Nike paid €22.5 million for the honour of making (and selling) PSG their shirts, compared to the €4 million they paid Monaco.

On the plus side Monaco, for once, had not sold any stars. Fabio Coentrão had returned to Real Madrid, Ricardo Carvalho had retired, and the peripatetic Vagner Love swiftly moved on to Turkey, but none of Jardim's key players had been lured away. There were also some useful signings, especially in defence, with the arrivals of Djibril Sidibé from Lille, Kamil Glik (after a good Euro 2016 with Poland) from Torino, and Benjamin Mendy from Marseille. In addition Falcao, after two miserable years on loan in England, was back, though neither player nor club seemed sure whether this was a good thing or not.

Crucially, the Colombian started well, scoring in both legs as Monaco beat Fenerbahce, of Istanbul, in the first of two hurdles Monaco needed to negotiate to reach the Champions League. In Ligue 1, however, ASM found themselves 2–0 down at home to Guingamp in their opening game. An 84th-minute goal from Bernardo Silva, back after injury prevented him taking part in Portugal's Euro 2016 triumph, earned a draw and changed the mood music. Monaco went on to win their next six matches, sweeping past Spain's Villarreal to reach the Champions League and beating PSG 3–1 in the principality en route to topping Ligue 1.

Defeat to neighbours Nice, who were proving a surprise package, not least as striker Mario Balotelli was starring for them, knocked Monaco off the summit, but from then on Jardim's team seemed jet-propelled. In Europe they topped a tricky group, beating Tottenham home and away (the latter match being played at Wembley) and also seeing off Bayer Leverkusen and CSKA Moscow. In France they averaged more than three goals a game as they reached the winter break just behind Nice.

Jardim, in one of several masterstrokes, had made Falcao captain. The Colombian relished the honour and responsibility, the 31-year-old helping guide a young team (with an average age of twenty-four) and seemingly reinvigorated by their youthful enthusiasm in return. At the end of the season Vadim Vasilyev said of the returning star:

> In England he was not handled correctly. Either they did not want or did not know how to do it. If you take a player who comes from a serious injury you cannot expect him to play from day one. You cannot. You cannot. It's just impossible. So if you really want this player you need to give him time and build him up gradually – five minutes, ten minutes, fifteen minutes. Stop – 'how do you feel?' Then give him more playing time. You launch him. But this was not the case at either of the two clubs. He played one, two games then 'boom' – out. That's it. It was a mistake. For us, this experience has made him stronger and right now he's a real captain, a real leader.

Falcao was initially paired with another returning loanee, Valère Germain, at the head of a 4-4-2 formation that featured Bernardo Silva and Thomas Lemar on the flanks, Mendy and Sidibé overlapping, and Fabinho and Tiemoue

Bakayoko in central midfield. 'There are a lot of attackers in the squad and I think 4-4-2 is the best system for us,' said Jardim on the eve of the season. 'In this system we have dynamism wide and get the crosses in.'

Monaco did not just score heavily, with Glik impressing, they were also solid at the back, conceding 40 per cent fewer goals than in the previous season. There was depth, too, with the likes of Moutinho and Nabil Dirar playing strong supporting roles.

To mark his first five years at ASM, Dmitry Rybolovlev gave two of his rare interviews, to *Aujourd'hui en France* and *Monaco-Matin*. Reflecting on his stewardship, the Russian said:

When I took over the club, in December 2011, the team was bottom of Ligue 2. Since earning promotion back to Ligue 1 in 2013, the club has finished in the top three every season, played in Europe and was even among the top eight clubs in Europe in 2015. I think we can call that a success. For sure, we need to improve further to win trophies, but I'm very proud to have taken over AS Monaco to restore the prestige the club deserves. I intend to stay at the helm of AS Monaco for a long time yet, because it gives me great pleasure. I want the club to qualify for Europe every year, preferably the Champions League. But I don't want to be content with second or third place. I'd like to win the French league title again. It will be difficult this year as PSG still have considerable financial clout. But I allow myself to dream and am convinced that if we work hard, we can achieve that goal.

Progress towards that target was swift. In their first league game of 2017 Monaco went along the coast to thrash Marseille 4–1 in the Stade Velodrome (the match that prompted Emmanuel Macron's despair in 'Macron: Behind the Scenes of a Victory').

That took them back to the top of Ligue 1, a position they retained to the end of the season, going the final twenty games unbeaten. In the cups they were bested by PSG, losing in the final of the Coupe de la Ligue 4–1 and in the semi-finals of the Coupe de France 5–0. But in the league Silva secured a draw in the capital with a last-minute goal, a result that prevented PSG drawing level. From then on Monaco pulled away, finishing eight points clear of their wealthy rivals, with Nice coming third, nine points further adrift. With 107 goals Monaco broke the French league record (and conceded only thirty-one); their haul of ninety-five points was one short of the record (set by PSG the previous year).

It was, Prince Albert told Canal+, 'an extraordinary season'. He added: 'Four and a half years ago we were in Ligue 2, now we find ourselves champions of France. This group is extraordinary, talented and very good-spirited, led by a great coach. It is a work of a whole team, but also of the staff, and the supporters.'

'This is the most important trophy of my life as a coach,'

said Jardim. 'Winning a championship in a team that is not a favourite is a great trophy. Monaco winning the league is the equivalent of PSG winning it four times. I think it's the best season in Monaco's history: the league title, final of the Coupe de la Ligue, semi-finals of the Coupe de France and the Champions League.'

Ah yes, the Champions League. Not content with dismissing Spurs Monaco put out Pep Guardiola's Manchester City, winning a thrilling tie on away goals after a 6–6 aggregate score. That was the moment when Europe suddenly realised there was something special happening in the principality.

In particular, the Continent's big clubs had cottoned on to the arrival of a new star: teenager Kylian Mbappé, recruited at fifteen from the national system. Having been given the occasional outing in the autumn, the eighteen-year-old became Falcao's regular partner from February, his pace, trickery, and *sangfroid* in front of goal astounding fans and pundits alike. He scored a dozen goals in the title run-in, and made an impact in Europe scoring home and away against Manchester City and, in the quarter-finals, against Borussia Dortmund. Two of those goals came in Germany, in a tie that was delayed for twenty-four hours after a roadside bomb attack on the Dortmund team bus which put one player, Marc Baltra, in hospital with a broken wrist. Terrorism was feared but it transpired that the culprit was a speculator seeking to make a near-€4 million profit from a fall in Dortmund's shares.

Juventus, streetwise, hard-edged, and smart, ended Monaco's European dream at the semi-final stage, winning 2–1 in Turin and 2–0 in the principality. But the Champions League run had always been seen as a bonus; winning the domestic title was the prime target and Monaco celebrated rapturously. Mbappé led his teammates into Jardim's post-match press conference and doused him with a huge container of water and ice. The players then delivered a ringing rendition of 'Ole, Ole, Ole, Ole'.

'We're a bunch of mates who enjoy playing football together,' was Mbappé's description of Monaco's secret.

Their youthfulness – at twenty-four Sidibé was nicknamed 'Uncle Djib' while thirty-two-year-old goalkeeper Danijel Subašic split the squad into 'adults' (himself, Falcao and Glik) and 'talented kids' – did create a *joie de vivre*. The players marked their triumph by dyeing their heads and hair in club colours for the final match, and the club, after a reception with Prince Albert, staged a victory party featuring hip-hop superstar 50 Cent.

But as with all parties, there was a hangover. The vultures were already circling. Prince Albert said: 'I think this team has a tremendous talent with young people who can still progress [but] they cannot all stay. There will necessarily be some departures.'

Dmitri Rybolovlev, who said he felt 'happiness, emotion and an immense satisfaction' at the title success, admitted he would not prevent players from moving on:

We are not here to decide in the place of men, block them, tell them yes or no. We have no budget problem and we are not forced to sell, but the day when a player or coach wants to leave, it's just unimaginable to keep him against his wishes. We are not Real Madrid or Barcelona or Manchester. Everyone has to cross the road in his career to go even higher. You do not keep a man against his will. In business, if you go against the market and against the trends, you will always lose. After, if someone goes, this is not our initiative. It's a decision of the player, not the club.

The owner's right-hand man, Vadim Vasilyev, agreed, but said in interviews that it was the price of success:

To have players coveted by other clubs, these are good difficulties. Every club official would like to be in my shoes. I think there will be quite a few [offers]. We have done a great job, we have fantastic quality players. The idea is to extend the contracts of most players, to keep them, even if there'll obviously be some departures. Maybe some of them they will ask to leave. We are a fantastic club but with the big names it's difficult for the players to resist – how many players can play for the biggest clubs in the world who always go to the semi-finals and finals of the Champions League? A player also understands that maybe next year he will not get such an offer. So this is our handicap because we are not on this level. We are not on a level par with the biggest clubs in the world so in this case we can't resist financially to a certain extent. But we also have to understand the psychology of the player. If he wants to continue his journey with us then we will do everything to keep him.

There will be some departures, but we will definitely not let half a team go because we want to keep the team competitive for next year. It will be difficult to repeat such an exceptional season. But we will try and keep the title.

One key player, Falcao, swiftly accepted the offer of a new contract, but younger players had dreams to pursue. Silva went to Manchester City for a staggering €50 million (£43.5 million), plus a potential €20 million in add-ons. That gave Monaco a €34.25 million profit in two seasons. Mbappé, Mendy, Lemar, and Bakayoko were also in demand. Real Madrid, and then Arsenal, had huge €100 million bids for Mbappé turned down. Speculation grew that he could be persuaded to remain.

There was also the question of whether Jardim would stay. The 42-year-old's contract had two years to run. 'We will try and extend Leonardo Jardim's contract,' Vasilyev told the *Téléfoot* TV programme. 'He never said he wants to leave.'

The good news came in June as Jardim extended his deal to 2020. He said he had 'the ambition to continue this project and continue to grow the club with the same passion that drives us since the beginning.'

Even as the team was being raided, replacements were

being sourced. Half the Silva cash was diverted to Brussels with the recruitment of twenty-year-old Youri Tielemans from Belgian champions Anderlecht. 'Youri has won the Belgian league title, been named player of the season, and made it to the quarter-finals of the Europa League,' said Vasilyev.

He was on the radar of some very big clubs, but it's at AS Monaco that he has chosen to continue his development. We are delighted with his decision, as it shows that our project is more attractive than ever, and is recognition of a certain savoir-faire.

His arrival is fully in line with our strategy of signing talented young players. That strategy, which saw us win the French title and lifted us into the top four clubs in Europe, is bearing fruit.

We will continue working to build a squad with big talents every year. Youri coming in now, with the season only just over, reflects our strong commitment to building an ambitious and very competitive team for next season.

An even more significant purchase in Belgium was that of an entire club, Cercle Brugge. Founded in the nineteenth century and three-time Belgian champions, they were now in the second tier and had fallen on hard times financially. An AS Monaco communiqué said:

This project is part of the AS Monaco development strategy

in relation to young talents. The club will benefit from the savoir-faire of the 'Belgian school' while respecting the traditions and values of Cercle Brugge, a historic Belgian football club. This project will allow young players from the Monaco academy to take an extra step in their progression from the reserve team to the first team squad. The first aim will be to do everything we can to take the club back to the 1st division of Belgian football.

Long-term thinking was also in evidence with the appointment of a successor to Luis Campos, Monaco's 'super scout'. Antonio Cordon was lured from Spain where he had spent sixteen years at Villarreal, a club that has long outperformed its budget. Cordon explains his new role was more focused on the first team than at Villarreal, with a group of fourteen scouts under his command reviewing, in the flesh and via video, more than 200 matches a week. Cordon also brought in a compatriot, Juanjo Morillas, as nutritionist to oversee the diet of players from first team to the academy. 'We are trying to get the younger ones to know what they have to eat and to take care of their eating habits from a young age,' said Cordon.

Steadily every aspect of the club is being refined. If Monaco is to continue to not only compete with, but also beat PSG at home, and the likes of Arsenal, Manchester City and Borussia Dortmund in Europe, no element can be ignored.

CHAPTER 16

A CAPTAIN WITH NO QUALMS

Nothing about Dmitry Rybolovlev is commonplace. And so, when I asked him, at the end of a three-hour interview, about his vision for the future, his answer inevitably needed to be further deciphered: 'I have thought about it a lot, and I'm now close to making a decision. I have two options for the next interesting project that I could get involved in,' he says. 'But I'm still hesitating. One thing is sure: once I decide, there will be no regrets or looking back.'[114]

This modus operandi, almost a mantra, can sometimes be surprising, disturbing, or irritating. But it's certainly the way this Russian billionaire operates. He turned fifty on 22 November 2016, one of life's crossroads. On his path from Perm to Monaco, he has experienced a multitude of events. He's not a saint – far from it – but his aura, although sometimes diminished, with his eleven months in prison or his turbulent divorce, continues to shine brightly.

---

114   Interview with the author.

'Does an angel watch over me?' he asks.

Well, there have certainly been many unexpected events in my life, and I have always emerged unscathed, even from the most difficult situations. The most important thing I have learned is that you must be true to yourself. You shouldn't change depending on the situation or as a tactic. But continue to follow your path.

His lawyer, Tetiana Bersheda, who knows him better than most, said:

He once told me that: 'If you are pessimistic, you won't succeed in business.' At the beginning of our collaboration, he also said something to me that I have never forgotten: 'Throughout our lifetime we will fall, get burned, and hurt ourselves. But we have to get up and keep going. If after you have been burned, you stop trusting people, life isn't worth living.'

He always looks out for the positive things, because in spite of what has happened, he believes in human nature. After all he has been through, you would think he'd have lost his compassion and humanity and become hardened. But he is still attentive to others, touched by their problems. When you spend time with him, you forget who he really is. Although he is the capitalist businessman par excellence, with an astounding ability to anticipate and synthesise things, he is resolutely positive. When he chooses a path, he sticks to it. But that doesn't prevent him from doubting sometimes. He is demanding but fair. When he asks a question, you have to reply and think at the same speed as he does. In fact, even when he is silent, he's thinking. He does it constantly; he never switches off his brain![115]

Dmitry Rybolovlev is full of certainty. As steady as a rock, he is like a captain standing firm at the helm during a storm. He throws emotion, angst, and anything that might slow him down overboard. He gives you the impression of having foreseen everything. Even his future: according to two Russian sources, a cemetery near a chapel in Moscow has already been chosen.

He cultivates a sense of mystery, given the extent to which he snubs journalistic efforts. Loath to speak about himself, he has settled in a luxurious penthouse in Monaco. But he has seen his reputation improve since becoming the head of the Monegasque club and having to embody the glamour of the principality. It is football that has made him a public figure (even though he refuses to take on after-sales service) and not his success in business or his work as an accident and emergency doctor, who had believed he was destined to follow in the footsteps of his physician father. There has from time to time been speculation that he might depart from AS

---

115   Interview with the author.

Monaco, because of his finances, health, or a desire for new challenges. But for the time being he is securely attached to the Rock, this glittering village where everyone secretly harbours hopes for their neighbour's downfall.

'The club has been restructured, the engine has been fine-tuned and is going in the right direction. The model is a good one. Now, we need results!' he says, speaking before the remarkable 2016–17 season. He smiles, and adds: 'Paris Saint-Germain is a serious obstacle. Maybe they need to win the Champions League so that the Qataris will be satisfied and calm down a little.'

The way he leads Monaco is a tribute to his character and philosophy. Absent from the media frontline, he leads with an iron hand, making all the crucial decisions. Football is an industry based on live performances, but it is an industry first of all, with its own economy. There is not much room for Russian romanticism in his life. Rybolovlev is pragmatic; he thinks first in terms of business, whereas so many other club executives get carried away with the excitement and give in to their urges.

In this regard, the case of Anthony Martial is symptomatic. After the massive investment once promotion to Ligue 1 was secured, demonstrated by the princely recruitment in summer 2013 with a European-highest figure of €165 million spent, Monaco modified their strategy, confronted with Financial Fair Play and their limited revenue. The club has reconfigured itself to manage the loss of four or five key players at each pre-season, becoming more of a transit zone, exhibition stand, and springboard for later re-sale with enhanced value, instead of a place to sign up for the long term. Cynical? More like realistic. Some are not in agreement with this approach. Football idealists have expressed their views, arguing that the sporting aspect of the Monaco project is an illusion. But few are the clubs that can behave otherwise, and always with Rybolovlev, market law will prevail. He is neither a philanthropist nor a patron: above all, he is a businessman.

On 31 August 2015, although considered indispensable, the nineteen-year-old forward Martial was sold to Manchester United. Monaco, even after Lyon's cut, gained a minimum €40 million and a potential €64 million. Was the player, who only a few hours later was called up for his French cap, worth it? Football is irrational and opinions varied from week to week. A relative unknown when he arrived in England, and met with much scepticism, Martial was soon seen as the next Thierry Henry after some fancy footwork and an equalising goal at Old Trafford against Liverpool in his first match, where he came on as a substitute. He followed that up with a double the following week at Southampton.

But then he struggled, as Louis van Gaal, followed by José Mourinho, tried to revive a side that had experienced an unexpectedly prolonged hangover after the departure of Old Trafford's Godfather, Sir Alex Ferguson. Martial was dropped from the starting squad and consequently lost his place in the French team. For United's biggest match of 2016–17, the

Europa League final, he was granted just six minutes as a late substitute, prompting further doubts about his future at United.

However, his place in Monaco's story is secure. In 2017, Ranieri was asked about his best signing. It was expected he would say Frank Lampard, a wonderful signing for Chelsea, or N'Golo Kanté, the remarkable midfielder who inspired Leicester City and Chelsea to consecutive Premier League titles, making the former club a £30 million profit along the way. Ranieri surprised when he said: 'I think the best was Martial for Monaco. We buy him for €5 million and sell for €60 million.'

Which is why Rybolovlev didn't hesitate for a second to sell the striker when Manchester United came knocking. He refuses to accept that losing money and deepening budget deficits in football is inescapable. Profitability shouldn't be pure illusion. While his compatriot Roman Abramovich, owner of Chelsea, did indeed win the Champions League in 2012, over nine seasons he has invested 17 per cent of his personal fortune into the London club (€1.2 billion for players' salaries and €620 million in transfers). At the opening of the 2015–16 season, Monaco had recorded twenty arrivals and thirty departures, resulting in a positive balance sheet. It's more about investing than sporting logic.

Rybolovlev is not a dreamer. He never forgets that business is business, even if that mars the club's image, interferes with his ambition, or … annoys *L'Équipe*. The daily sports newspaper printed on 1 September 2015 a column entitled 'A Taste of Ashes', following a double blow for ASM – who were prevented from advancing in the Champions League by Valencia in the play-offs (generating a shortfall of €20 million) and a thrashing at home against PSG – which virulently proclaimed its total incomprehension. 'It is fair that sometimes this game punishes those that are scornful of it. ... Everywhere else (more or less), football is the objective and investment is a way of achieving it. For Monaco, investment is the objective and football is a way of achieving it.'

From December 2011, when Rybolovlev became chairman of AS Monaco, to the end of May 2017, Monaco's transfer turnover has been €746 million. Of that, €411 million has been spent, with €335 million recouped in sales. Those figures, however, hide the reality that since the summer of 2014, the focus has been on purchasing talent that can be sold on at a profit, rather than buying ready-made football stars.

Monaco is not just one of Rybolovlev's whims. Paradoxically, that's what some people reproached him for when he sold Martial to United, but he has always known how to yield profit from his assets and 'commodities', whether it be potassium or football players. Secretive and cerebral, entirely resilient towards all forms of pressure, uplifted by competition, consistently reserved, impervious to criticism, and only appreciative of effectiveness, the Russian (and I have been able to observe it first-hand) does not operate through seduction. He doesn't lay on the charm or complicate matters.

He doesn't try to seem nice (which is what actually makes him seem nice).

He doesn't shy away from speaking with people, but he raises an invisible wall, a wall that only comes down in private, particularly with his parents and his daughters. Because of his background, his strict personality, his millions of euros, his natural aptitude for business, his sometimes perverse pleasure that he derives from the sense of fear he can provoke, he provokes a variety of strong reactions; these things will continue to accompany him, no matter what we think of his extraordinary trajectory. This book has tried to paint the exhaustive portrait of a man who is by no means a hardly mundane personality, at one with the evolution of his homeland – a kind of mix between controversial retail tycoon Phillip Green and Citizen Kane, the eponymous central character in Orson Welles's masterpiece about power, fortune, solitude, and the passage of time.

The Rybolovlev story is also the story of a lover of football; a sport he discovered later in life, while among the spectators at Stamford Bridge. The tale of someone who is passionate about strategy on the field and who is caught up in the decorum inherent to its role.

He is a man who, when there are few cheers from supporters in Stade Louis II, says: 'It's not a problem. I experience so many emotions, I wouldn't even notice if I was alone in the stadium ...' A man who, while travelling in South America, was invited by the president of River Plate, from whom he bought Lucas Ocampos, to watch the feverish derby between Boca Juniors and River in Buenos Aires. He mixes happily with the likes of Karl-Heinz Rummenigge, the former German World Cup runner-up, now a key player in European football, given his role at Bayern Munich; Andrea Agnelli, the young chairman of Juventus; Michel Platini, a legendary player and, before his downfall, influential administrator; and Jorge Mendes, the renowned agent. Rybolovlev finds the vicissitudes and pitfalls of the discipline amusing, such as an addiction to the game, Adriano Galliani-style.

Galliani, the vice president of AC Milan, had piled on the pressure for a meeting with Rybolovlev and, when he finally met the Russian at a dinner, he made him an offer: the duo Kevin-Prince Boateng and Stephan El Shaarawy for €60 million. Rybolovlev had no intention of accepting, but was happy to hear out his fellow guest, a close acquaintance of Silvio Berlusconi. The next day, alerted by Galliani, *La Gazzetta dello Sport* plastered on its front page: 'Monaco Offers €60 Million for Boateng and El Shaarawy!' As an aside: the following season, on 13 July 2015, the Italian international forward of Egyptian origin was lent to the principality's club for one year with a buyout option. Six months, twenty-four matches and three goals later, 'the Pharaoh' signed up with AS Roma, and Jardim's side found a replacement in the form of Brazilian Vagner Love.

After long months of defiance and conflict with the Federation and the national League, Rybolovlev has become more involved with the French football family, from Jean-Michel Aulas to Bernard Caïazzo. Despite the presidents of Ligue 1 still only seeing him sporadically – although they continue to communicate with the affable Vasilyev – his relationships with these other football heavyweights have stabilised.

'Dmitry thrives in Monaco. After having lived in Russia and Switzerland, he has found the country where he is most at ease,' says Vasilyev. 'AS Monaco's ambition, despite our limited revenue from tickets and sponsors, is to reach the podium [top three] each year and to make a good showing in the European competitions. We have big dreams.'[116]

A resident of the smallest independent state in the world after the Vatican and the most densely populated behind Singapore, Rybolovlev wants to be a Monegasque citizen. 'Football broke the ice, bringing Dmitry and Prince Albert closer together. For example, Dmitry was at the baptism of the Prince's twins. Their relationship has evolved,' claims Vasilyev, as if reacting to the frequent allegations of strained relations with the Palace, which is viscerally attached to the club.

The truth? It probably lies somewhere in-between. Our multiple requests for an interview, by all means possible, were courteously declined by HSH the Prince. A close associate of both Albert II and Rybolovlev was asked to give his opinion on the real nature of their relationship. He replied: 'Meditate on this expression: "The Lord moves in mysterious ways."'

---

116 Interview with the author.

The adventurous son of Perm in the Ural Mountains, who has become one of the principality's eminent figures, surely still has more adventures in store. Fuelled by challenges and ambition, and driven by a continual need to reinvent himself, he plays this sentence over and over again in his mind like a refrain: 'Fear and business are not compatible.'[117]

---

117   Interview with the author.

TIMELINE:
DMITRY RYBOLOVLEV AND AS MONACO

2011

May   Monaco are relegated to Ligue 2.

June   Dmitri Rybolovlev rebuffed in attempt to buy
           Monaco.

September Laurent Banide sacked as coach, Marco Simone
           hired.

December   Rybolovlev buys Monaco (now twentieth in
           Ligue 2).

2012

January   Ten players signed including Danijel Subašic,
           Nacer Barazite, Nabil Dirar, Ibrahima Touré. ASM
           win their first match of the Rybolovlev era at Istres.

May   French President Francois Hollande takes office.
Monaco finish eighth in Ligue 2.

Summer   Claudio Ranieri replaces Simone as coach.

Signings include Argentinian Lucas Ocampos (€11 million, Ligue 2 record).

September   Hollande announces 75 per cent super tax.

December   Super tax rate cut to 50 per cent.

2013

March   League declares all clubs must have their headquarters in France.

May   At Nice airport, Noël Le Graët demands €200 million fee for Monaco remaining outside the French tax system. Rybolovlev refuses. Monaco appeal the league decision to the Council of State.

May   Monaco promoted after leading Ligue 2 from start to finish.

Summer   Michel Denisot brokers meeting at Le Cinq, Paris. Rybolovlev again rebuffs €200 million request.

Radamel Falcao is signed from Atletico Madrid to Monaco for a record-breaking French fee of €60 million. Also signed are James Rodriguez (€25 million), Joao Moutinho (€45 million), Ricardo Carvalho, and Fabinho (initially on loan).

2014

January   Falcao injured during the Coupe de France and is out for the season.

League and Monaco agree that the tax compensation fee should be cut to €50 million.

May   Monaco finish second behind PSG.

UEFA fine nine clubs, including PSG and Manchester City, for breaking financial fair play regulations.

Summer   Ranieri replaced by Leonardo Jardim. Rodriguez sold to Real Madrid (€80 million), Yannick Ferreira Carrasco to Atletico Madrid (€20 million), Geoffrey Kondogbia bought from Sevilla (€20 million), and Aymen Abdennour from Toulouse (€15 million).

August   Falcao loaned to Manchester United (€10 million).

December Hollande abandons 75 per cent super tax.

2015

February   Monaco lose on penalties to Bastia in semi-final of Coupe de France.

April   Monaco reach Champions League quarter-final, losing to Juventus, having knocked out Arsenal en route.

May   Monaco finish third in Ligue 1 behind PSG and Lyon.

May   UEFA fine Monaco €13 million for breaking financial fair play regulations, and enforce restrictions on squad size and spending.

July   Courts rule €50 million fee 'illicit'. Monaco do not have to pay anything to keep their head-quarters in the principality.

Summer   Fábio Coentrão signs on loan from Real Madrid.

Layvin Kurzawa sold to PSG (€24 million), Kondogbia sold to Inter (€40 million), and Falcao loaned to Chelsea.

August   Monaco knocked out of the Champions League by Valencia, who buy Abdennour (€30 million). Martial sold to Manchester United (£50 million rising to £80 million). Berbatov released. Window spending €70 million but raises €200 million.

2016

May   Monaco again finish third in Ligue 1 behind PSG and Lyon.

Summer Falcao returns.

2017

May   Monaco KO'd in Champions League semi-finals by Juventus after a run that includes victories against Tottenham, Manchester City, and Borussia Dortmund.

May   Monaco win Ligue 1; first title since 2000.

June   Bernardo Silva sold to Manchester City (€50), but Jardim signs contract extension.

Falcao signs a new three-year contract extension committing himself to Monaco until 2020.

ACKNOWLEDGEMENTS

Spasiba to Sergey, the driving force behind the project, who, in all languages and with a smile, was able to unlock doors.

Thanks to both Andreys: the first for the wanderings around the cathedral Basile-le-Bienheureux and the visit to the Pushkin Museum in Moscow; and the second for tasting pelmenyi in Perm and the discovery of the labour camp Perm-36.

Thanks to the Kartanos father and son for their welcome and skewers in Lefkada.

Thanks also to Bruno, Alex, Willy, John, Jean-Marc, Danielle, Laurence, and Greg, and thanks to Géraldine, Martin, and Amélie for their title proposals.